QUEENSLAND

BRUCE ELDER

NEW
HOLLAND

This edition first published in 2001
by New Holland Publishers (UK) Ltd
London • Cape Town • Sydney • Auckland
First edition published in 1997
10 9 8 7 6 5 4 3 2 1

Garfield House, 86 Edgeware Road
London W2 2EA
United Kingdom

80 McKenzie Street
Cape Town 8001
South Africa

14 Aquatic Drive
Frenchs Forest, NSW 2086
Australia

218 Lake Road
Northcote, Auckland
New Zealand

Distributed in the USA by
The Globe Pequot Press
Connecticut

ISBN 185974 725 6

Commissioning Editor: Tim Jollands
Manager Globetrotter Maps: John Loubser
Managing Editor: Thea Grobbelaar
Editors: Tarryn Berry, Joanne Holliman
Picture Researchers: Sonya Meyer, Vicki Hastrich
Design and DTP: Lellyn Creamer, Sonya Cupido
Cartographers: Elaine Fick, William Smuts

Reproduction by Hirt & Carter (Pty) Ltd, Cape Town
Printed and bound in Hong Kong by Sing Cheong
Printing Co. Ltd

Although every effort has been made to ensure
accuracy of facts, telephone and fax numbers in this
book, the publishers will not be held responsible for
changes that occur at the time of going to press.

Photographic Credits:
Bruce Elder: pages 45, 48, 108, 114, 115, 116 (bottom);
Anthony Johnson: pages 4, 9, 10, 12, 20, 23, 30, 33
(bottom), 37, 38, 52, 76, 83, 90 (top), 96 (bottom); **Ian
Lever:** pages 118, 119; **NHAIL:** pages 33 (top), 35, 39,
42, 59, 61, 67 (bottom), 88, 116 (top); **NHAIL/Shaen
Adey:** pages 3, 4, title page, pages 6, 7, 13, 14, 17, 18,
19, 21, 24, 25, 26, 27, 28, 29, 36, 46, 55 (top and bottom), 56, 57, 58, 67 (top), 68, 69, 70, 71, 72, 73, 79 (top
and bottom), 80, 81, 82, 84, 85, 90 (bottom), 92, 93, 94,
95, 96 (top), 98, 99, 102, 105 (top and bottom), 106, 107;
NHAIL/Anthony Johnson: cover, **NHAIL/Bruce
Elder:** pages 11, 22, 109; **NHAIL/ Denise Greig:** page
44; **Nick Rains:** page 112; **Robin Smith:** pages 8, 15.
[NHAIL: New Holland Australia Image Library]

Front Cover: *Whitehaven Beach (Whitsunday Island),
a beautiful tropical beach with 5km (3 miles) of soft
white sand.*
Title Page: *Coral cays, underwater coral gardens and
the peacefulness of snorkelling are all part of the tourist
appeal of the Great Barrier Reef.*

CONTENTS

1
Introducing Queensland

Queensland likes to think of itself as '**The Sunshine State**'. Tourist advertising declares that it is the state where it is 'beautiful one day – perfect the next'. This perception is based on the state's **magnificent coastal scenery,** which from Coolangatta on the New South Wales border to Cairns in far north Queensland is an almost non-stop collection of beautiful beaches, coral cays, tropical islands, and waters which are impossibly clear and blue. It also based on the amount of sunshine the state experiences with both coastal and inland areas enjoying long periods – particularly during the winter – when the sun shines day after day.

Of course the state is more complex than the tourist image it presents the world. Although predominantly tropical (most of the state lies to the north of the **Tropic of Capricorn** which crosses the coast at Rockhampton and passes through Longreach in the central west), the state covers a diverse and large domain. In winter the south can experience snow and sub-zero temperatures while the Gulf Savannah around the Gulf of Carpentaria and the area north of Townsville is so mild that it has become one of Australia's most popular winter destinations. In summer, while the Gold Coast and Sunshine Coast are recognised as desirable holiday destinations, the tropical rain and the presence of box jellyfish, make the Far North far from attractive.

Beyond the coastal plain and the Great Dividing Range the state slowly dries out until in the far west it becomes, at best, marginal land moving towards desert.

TOP ATTRACTIONS

*** Great Barrier Reef: a wonder of the world, with magnificent coral formations and exotic tropical fish.
*** Cape Tribulation and the Daintree Rainforest: tropical rainforest, lonely beaches and forest streams.
*** Fraser Island: world's largest sand island with freshwater lakes, tropical rainforests, long, flat beaches and huge sand dunes.
*** Stockman's Hall of Fame: excellent displays; designed around 'The Australian History Timeline.'

Opposite: *A tropical paradise in the Whitsundays, Hamilton Island.*

FACTS AND FIGURES

Population: In 1999 a total of 3,512,356 people lived in Queensland, most of whom lived along the coastal fringe.
Tourism: By 1996 more than 1.3 million overseas visitors, of whom 62 per cent came from Asia, where visiting Queensland each year.
Geography: Queensland covers 1,733,000km^2 (669,000 sq miles) and has 7400km (4600 miles) of coastline.
The Great Artesian Basin: The world's largest artesian basin, covering 1.7 million km^2 (650,000 sq miles) from the Gulf of Carpentaria to the state borders with NSW and SA.

In the Far North, beyond Cairns and around the coast to the border with the Northern Territory, it changes from impenetrable rainforest to low-grade tropical savanna and swampy, mangrove wetlands. Consequently the majority of the state's 3.5 million people prefer to live either in Brisbane or along the coast in large urban sprawls like the Gold Coast, the Sunshine Coast, and the major cities of Townsville, Bundaberg, Cairns and Rockhampton.

In the past 20 years Australians, particularly those living in New South Wales and Victoria, have tended to see Queensland as a mixture of **tropical paradise** and land of opportunity. This has resulted in significant 'migration'. Between 1991 and 1999 the state's population increased by 11.8 per cent. Many of these people were elderly and retired. They sought the warmer climate and moved to the fast-developing areas along the coast to the north and south of Brisbane. Many younger people, believing that Queensland offered good job opportunities, also moved to the state's south-eastern quarter.

Queensland is a modern, dynamic state. The wide variety of holiday choices – lazy, tropical days by the sea; frontier challenges (off the beaten track); tranquil rainforests and national parks; exotic wildlife and stunning scenery; and arts and culture to suit all tastes – has also made it Australia's premier holiday destination for overseas tourists.

Right: *The northern half of Queensland lies in the tropics. At the Rockhampton Information Centre a spire indicates the Tropic of Capricorn.*

THE LAND

Queensland is Australia's second largest state – only Western Australia is larger – and it has the **largest habitable area** in the country. It covers a total of 1,733,000km² (699,000 sq miles) in the north-eastern corner of the continent and has over 7400km (4600 miles) of coastline stretching from the headland and beaches of Coolangatta and the Gold Coast north to Cape York and south and west around the Gulf of Carpentaria. When the islands around the coast – most notably the Whitsundays, Fraser Island, the islands on the eastern edge of Moreton Bay and in the Gulf – are added, the state's coastline is 9800km (6100 miles).

Above: *Behind the highly developed Gold Coast the escarpment rises to the cool, subtropical hinterland around Mt Tamborine. It is an area of waterfalls, gift shops and tea houses.*

The state is cut in half by the **Tropic of Capricorn** which passes close to Rockhampton on the coast and the town of Longreach inland.

The basic topographic variations occur from east to west. Most of the **coastal area** is a fertile strip of land which lies between the coast and the Great Dividing Range. Historically, the coast has been one of the state's main agricultural regions. The waters are rich with fish and crustaceans. The slopes of the Great Dividing Range were an important source of valuable tropical timber and the alluvial coastal plains have been ideal for tropical crops such as sugarcane, pineapples, mangoes, bananas, and pawpaws.

The **Great Dividing Range** starts about 200km (125 miles) south of Cape York and runs in a series of low-lying ranges and tablelands all the way down the eastern coastline. In many places it rises sharply from the coastline. The roads from Cairns to Kuranda and from Cairns to the Atherton Tablelands are typical. Numerous spectacular waterfalls tumble over the escarpment. A number of them – notably **Barron Falls** near Kuranda,

---

WHAT ARE QUEENSLANDERS LIKE?

There's a joke about Brisbane which captures the charm and uniqueness of Queensland people: When a stranger arrives in Perth the first question they are asked is 'Where do you come from?' In Adelaide, 'What church do you belong to?' In Melbourne, 'What school did you go to?' In Sydney, 'How much money have you got?'. But in Brisbane, someone in shorts and thongs throws a suntanned arm around the new chum's shoulder and says 'Come and have a drink'.

Above: *About 50km (31 miles) east of Ingham, lies the spectacular Wallaman Falls, the highest single drop waterfalls in Australia.*
Opposite: *Queensland's greatest natural attraction is the Great Barrier Reef with its beautiful, clear tropical waters and its coral gardens which stretch for thousands of kilometres down the coast from Cape York.*

the **Tully Falls** south of Cairns and the **Wallaman Falls** west of Ingham – are popular tourist attractions. The Wallaman Falls are the highest single drop falls in Australia tumbling 279m (893ft) down a sheer cliff.

The tablelands and slopes which lie west beyond the escarpment, are agriculturally rich. Around Atherton they are used as beef and dairy cattle country. This pattern of usage continues all the way down the state. The Stanthorpe–Texas area in south-east Queensland is known for its fine beef cattle.

The slopes slowly give way to the **great plains** of western Queensland which are marginal farming lands. It can rain less than 150mm (6in) a year at Birdsville. The area's cattle and sheep industries are sustained by the mighty **Cooper Creek** system (where water from the **monsoonal rains** of northern Queensland swells the river systems before disappearing into Lake Eyre in South Australia) and the **Great Artesian Basin**; hot, fresh mineral water which runs underground from Papua New Guinea to northern Victoria and rises from hundreds of metres below the surface.

Great Barrier Reef

The Great Barrier Reef is World Heritage listed area and is certainly the greatest of all Queensland's attractions. With a total area of 260,000km^2 (100,400 sq miles) it is the largest structure ever built by living creatures and, according to a *Trivial Pursuit* question, it can be seen from the moon. The reef stretches for over 2000km (1200 miles), from the mouth of the Fly River in Papua New Guinea, down the coast of Queensland, to **Lady Elliot Island** (latitude 24°S).

It is called the Great Barrier Reef but really it is an interconnecting series of some 2000 individual reefs and 71 coral islands. Within its boundaries are over 350 varieties of coral, some 4000 species of mollusc and an amazing 1200 varieties of fish.

Marine biologists recognise three clearly defined regions of the reef. The northernmost region (north of 16°S just below **Cooktown**) is characterised by shallow waters and continuous reef development to the edges of the continental shelf. This area is inaccessible to most tourists.

The central region (16°S–21°S) is deeper and there is little reef development near to the edge of the continental shelf where the water is 60m (196ft) deep. This is the area of the major tours. At **Cairns**, **Port Douglas** and **Whitsunday Islands** high-speed catamarans take visitors to moored platforms at the Outer Reef. The southern region (south of 21°S near **Mackay**) has abundant reef development out to the edge of the shelf.

It is difficult to place an actual age on the reef. Changing sea levels have meant periods of rapid growth and decay. During the Ice Age, when the level of the sea was considerably lower, large areas of the reef were exposed. Today only small areas are exposed at low tide.

The cliché 'underwater wonderland' is a remarkably apt description of the reef. Its formations from the huge red sea fans to the luxuriant coral cays are mesmerising and its fish, crustaceans, anemones and sea wasps (more commonly known as the box jelly fish) are mysterious, beautiful and exotic.

The economy of the reef is based primarily on tourism. There are now 24 **island resorts** including the coral cays of Heron, Green and Lady Elliot islands and the popular resorts of Magnetic Island near Townsville, Dunk Island, and the Whitsunday group which includes

> **UNUSUAL FACTS ABOUT THE GREAT BARRIER REEF**
>
> ● The Great Barrier Reef is the only thing on earth made by living creatures to be seen from the moon.
> ● The Great Barrier Reef Aquarium in Townsville has a living coral reef in captivity. The display is actually growing and developing.
> ● The maximum depth for the reef is over 60m (200ft) at the southern end of the reef.
> ● It has been estimated that the reef has more than 350 species of coral, 4000 species of mollusc and is home to more than 1200 species of fish (more than in the entire North Atlantic).

SHARKS AND BOX JELLYFISH

Two creatures most feared off the coast of Queensland are sharks and box jellyfish. Sharks abound in the warm tropical waters; however, the fear of a shark attack is largely unjustified. In the first 150 years of European settlement there were only 100 fatalities. It is simply a question of common sense. Do not swim in unpatrolled waters and not, under any circumstances, where signs warn of the danger of sharks. The box jellyfish is so deadly that from November through until April most of the beaches north of Townsville are not suitable for swimming. In some areas – beaches north of Cairns – stinger nets allow for swimming in the summer months.

Hayman Island, Hamilton Island, South Molle, Daydream, and Lindeman islands. Apart from swimming, sunbaking and sightseeing the reef's beauty attracts divers from all over the world. Beyond the reef deep sea fishing, particularly for black marlin, is popular. Over 60% of all tourists arriving in Australia nominate Queensland as their primary destination and the Great Barrier Reef is a vital part of this decision.

In the past 20 years the Great Barrier Reef area has undergone a development metamorphosis. In 1994 it had over 40 international hotels and tourist resorts, more than a dozen huge marinas, and a network of ancillary facilities such as casinos, charter cruises, sporting complexes, and hundreds of motels and restaurants.

Organisations like **FantaSea Cruises** in the Whitsundays and **Quicksilver** in Cairns–Port Douglas have built businesses on daily trips to the reef which provide opportunities to scuba dive and snorkel, to inspect the coral gardens from submersible boats, and to sit in underwater viewing bays and observe the tropical fish.

The reef is not an important commercial fishing region but it is fished for prawns, mud crabs, scallops and sand crabs. Local fishing fleets work mainly for the local restaurant trade.

Right: *Island resorts are dotted throughout the Whitsunday group. The resort on Hamilton Island is recognised as one of the best with luxury accommodation and restaurants.*
Opposite: *Each day cruises visit the Outer Reef beyond the Whitsundays. Here travellers can snorkel, scuba dive and travel across the coral gardens in submersibles.*

Since 1976 the Reef has been part of the **Great Barrier Reef Marine Park Authority**. In theory this has ensured its protection from exploitation. In practice no legislation can protect it from the ravages of the **crown of thorns starfish**, and periodic government murmuring about mineral exploration send shivers down the spines of the environmentalists.

Climate

Queensland is a state of great variations. From the north to the south it is equally divided by the **Tropic of Capricorn** (which is the beginning of the true tropics) and from the east to the west it moves from coastal conditions through mild mountain temperatures to harsh desert continentality.

In the south east, the Gold Coast, Brisbane and Sunshine Coast areas, the weather in winter is mild and pleasant and the summer tends to be hot and sticky.

Further north the winters are warm (certainly warm enough for swimming) but the summers are affected by **cyclonic conditions**. The greatest rainfall is between December and February and is commonly associated with serious cyclonic depressions which form in the

COMPARATIVE CLIMATE CHART	BRISBANE				ROCKHAMPTON				CAIRNS			
	SUM	AUT	WIN	SPR	SUM	AUT	WIN	SPR	SUM	AUT	WIN	SPR
	JAN	APR	JULY	OCT	JAN	APR	JULY	OCT	JAN	APR	JULY	OCT
MIN TEMP. °C	21	17	10	16	22	18	9	17	24	22	17	21
MAX TEMP. °C	29	26	21	26	31	29	23	30	32	29	26	29
MIN TEMP. °F	70	63	48	61	72	64	48	63	75	70	63	70
MAX TEMP. °F	84	79	70	79	88	84	73	84	88	84	79	84
HOURS OF SUN	8	7	7	8	8	7	7	7	7	6	7	9
RAINFALL mm	161	93	65	95	480	208	120	136	409	201	28	36
RAINFALL in	6	4	3	4	19	8	5	5	16	8	1	1

Above: *In the winter months visitors flock to the resorts along the north Queensland coast. The warm dry weather is ideal for swimming, sunbathing and relaxing.*

WHERE TO SEE THE FLORA

• **Daintree:** north of Cairns, still the state's best preserved stand of unspoilt tropical rainforest.
• **Carnarvon Gorge:** excellent diversity of subtropical eucalypts in an attractive setting.
• **Cunnamulla:** dry Artesian Basin region, scrubby growth interrupted by occasional gum trees with large areas cleared for grazing.
• **Birdsville:** west Queensland desert vegetation.

Pacific and come across the coast laden with rain. These conditions bring heavy rain to **Cape York** and the **Gulf of Carpentaria** and swell the rivers which run inland into western Queensland.

Beyond the coast the days become sunnier, the nights become colder and the rainfall decreases.

The far south west of the state experiences an average of over 10 hours sunshine a day and less than 150mm (6in) of rainfall a year.

Further east in the **Darling Downs** and on the low lying mountains around **Stanthorpe** and **Warwick** the winter temperatures can drop below freezing.

The state has built its tourist reputation on being **'The Sunshine State'**. This is an accurate description of the climate, particularly in the winter, spring and autumn months.

Plant Life

While the most potent image of Australia's plant life is the eucalypt, the **gum tree**, Queensland is more complex than this simple image. Certainly there are vast stands of eucalyptus in Queensland but the state's interest lies in the vast 'grey plains' of bush-like **mallee**

scrub which run from the Gulf of Carpentaria to the southwestern border. This grey scrub gives way to grasslands and finally desert.

Equally the most interesting vegetation on the coast is the rich diversity of rainforest which exists in the valleys of the Great Dividing Range. Here hoop pines, huge tree ferns, staghorns, liana vines and tall, straight eucalyptus grow densely, fed by the high rainfall and the strong tropical sunshine.

Of particular interest are the extensive **mangrove swamps** on the coastal edge. At many points these mangroves form a dense barrier between the sea and the land.

It has been estimated that Australia has some 20,000 species of flora which range from the tropical rainforests through mangroves, sclerophyll forests, savannas, mallee scrub and desert. Most of these species exist in Queensland.

The best way to appreciate this richness and diversity is to travel from the coast across to the western plains. A perfect journey would be from Cairns, south on the Kennedy Highway, and west to Mt Isa on the Flinders Highway.

TROPICAL RAINFOREST

At the beginning of the 19th century, before Europeans started cutting down the tropical rainforests, Queensland had Australia's only true tropical rainforest – extending from Cape York down the east coast to just south of modern-day Mackay. Today there are only pockets of true tropical rainforest. The most significant include the McIlwraith Ranges at the top end of Cape York; the area extending down the coast from Cooktown to Daintree; and the area behind the coast between Cairns and Cardwell – although greatly reduced by farming, they are still significant. The best place to experience Queensland's tropical rainforest is between Daintree and Cape Tribulation. The road is accessible and the forest is dense.

Left: *Huge tree ferns, such as these in the Atherton Tablelands near Millaa Millaa, are common in the tropical rainforest areas of north Queensland.*

Animal Life

Isolated from Southeast Asia, Australia has developed its own, unique animal species. Animals such as platypuses, kangaroos, wallabies, koalas and spiny anteaters have given Australia the reputation of strange and exotic animals.

The monotremes (egg-laying mammals), represented by the platypus and echidna (spiny anteater), and the marsupials – ranging from kangaroos and wallabies through to wombats, koalas, numbats and phalangers – can sometimes be seen in the wild but can, more readily, be seen in zoos and wildlife parks along the Queensland coast.

The kangaroo population of western Queensland is so vast that professional, government-licensed kangaroo hunters keep the numbers down. It is common to be confronted, particularly at dusk, by kangaroos who leap across roads and bump into passing vehicles causing their death and serious damage to the vehicle. Between Blackall and Charleville it is possible to see over 1000 dead kangaroos every 100km (60 miles).

Queensland has more than its share of dangerous creatures. It has large numbers of poisonous snakes, sharks are common in the coastal waters, the deadly box jellyfish in the summer north of Gladstone means that ocean swimming is impossible, and the extremely dangerous estuarine crocodile which lives in the rivers of the Far North and the Gulf.

In certain areas – notably on Fraser Island – the dingo (native dog) can be seen. They are wild animals and should not be fed or played with. While there is no evidence that dingoes will attack humans, it is known that, like domestc dogs, they can attack if provoked or hungry.

WHERE TO SEE NATIVE FAUNA

Queensland has many parks and sanctuaries where native animals can be viewed.
- **The Lone Pine Koala Sanctuary**, Brisbane, (09:30–17:00): ideal for inspecting koalas.
- **Currumbin Sanctuary**, Gold Coast, (08:00–17:00): large and comprehensive, with parrots and rosellas.
- **David Fleay Wildlife Park**, Burleigh Heads, Gold Coast, (09:00–17:00): a wide range of fauna including crocodiles, wallabies, koalas and emus.
- **Green Island Underwater Observatory**: excellent for both coral and tropical fish.

HISTORY IN BRIEF
Before the Arrival of Europeans

It is not known exactly when the first Aborigines arrived in Australia. Current theories tend towards around 60,000 B.P. (Before Present) and conjecture that they probably reached the coasts of the Northern Territory and Western Australia by a combination of walking and island hopping through the Indonesian archipelago. Certainly by 38,000 B.P. Aborigines had reached as far south as the Swan River in Western Australia and it is reasonable to assume that they had moved across and settled in Queensland. By 32,000 B.P. they were in western NSW and by 24,000 B.P. they had reached Tasmania.

The most likely date for the arrival of Aborigines in Queensland is probably around 45,000 B.P. Although no artefacts have been found to support this date, its proponents argue that a huge increase in charcoal residue from this time suggests extensive burning off of the area around Chillagoe in north Queensland.

The oldest known Aboriginal settlement in Queensland is located at **Kenniff Cave** on Mt Moffatt station in the south. In 1962, only a little over a decade after the development of radiocarbon dating, prehistorians dated the site as being 16,000 years old. It was an ideal site being both large and well protected. In the cave the excavators discovered paintings of boomerangs, an axe and a shield and stencil paintings of hands and feet. When the cave was excavated to a depth of 3.3m (11ft) more than 800 artefacts were found. Further radiocarbon dating revealed that the first occupants of the cave had arrived nearly 19,000 years ago.

Another important site is **Walkunder Arch Cave** at Chillagoe – the oldest found in north Queensland and dated to 18,000 B.P. It is of particular interest because there is evidence that the occupants of the cave were adept at using termite mounds as a

Opposite: *Kangaroos abound in western Queensland. At dawn and dusk they can be seen beside the roads. In captivity their placid disposition makes them a vital part of wildlife parks.* **Below:** *Queensland has a large number of important Aboriginal sites, including the Cathedral Cave in the Carnarvon National Park, where ancient hand paintings can be observed.*

Opposite: Captain James Cook spent six weeks at the site of Cooktown repairing the Endeavour *after it had been damaged on the Great Barrier Reef. The James Cook Historical Museum commemorates this first, short-lived European settlement on Australian soil.*

form of fuel. There is also evidence of a *Diprotodon*, an extinct animal which was like a giant wombat. Important artefacts dating beyond 17,550 B.P. have also been discovered at **Colless Creek** north west of Mt Isa in the far west of Queensland.

Certainly by the time Europeans arrived, the whole of Queensland had been settled and distinct linguistic groups had developed quite independently from each other. Although larger groups regularly gathered to share bountiful food supplies and to engage in barter and social rituals, Aborigines in Queensland moved in relatively small groups and lived by hunting and gathering. Their culture was remarkably sophisticated. There is still evidence, both in terms of cave paintings and in terms of oral history, of the voyage of Willem Jansz's ship the *Duyfken* which sailed down the western coast of Cape York Peninsula in 1606.

HISTORICAL CALENDAR

c.40,000 B.P. Aborigines move into western Queensland.
1606 Willem Jansz sails around Cape York Peninsula.
1644 Abel Tasman explores Cape York and names it Carpentaria Land.
1770 Captain James Cook sails up coast and names entire area New South Wales.
1799 Captain Matthew Flinders sails up the coast and explores both Moreton and Hervey bays.
1823 John Oxley chooses Moreton Bay as a suitable site for a harsh penal colony.
1824 Settlement of 29 convicts, 1 overseer and Lieutenant Henry Miller establish penal colony at Redcliffe Point. Colony moves to Brisbane River after a few months.
1827 Alan Cunningham names Darling Downs and finds inland route to penal colony through Cunninghams Gap.
1839 Brisbane ceases to be a penal colony.
1840 First squatters reach the Darling Downs.
1842 First free settlers arrive at Moreton Bay.
1844 Both Ludwig Leichhardt and Sir Thomas Mitchell start exploring inland.
1859 Queensland proclaimed a separate colony from NSW.

1863 First kanakas from Pacific Islands arrive to work on sugar and cotton fields.
1867 Gold discovered at Gympie.
1884 Queensland administers southern part of New Guinea.
1889 Australian Labour Federation, later the Australian Labor Party, formed in Queensland.
1902 Brisbane proclaimed a city.
1915 ALP wins state election. They hold power until 1957.
1920 Qantas formed at Winton.
1922 Legislative Council (the Upper House) is abolished.
1923 Silver, lead and zinc found at Mt Isa.
1955 Bauxite discovered at Weipa.
1957 ALP loses election and Liberal–Country coalition came to power.
1961 Oil discovered at Moonie and coal mined at Moura.
1968 Johannes Bjelke-Petersen becomes Premier.
1981 Great Barrier Reef is World Heritage listed.
1989 ALP wins election after 32 years in Opposition.
1996 ALP loses to Coalition when by-election gives balance of power to Independent.
1998 ALP win government, led by Peter Beattie.

This life came to an abrupt halt when explorers and settlers pushed north from the colonial outpost of Sydney and started to settle Queensland.

Arrival of Europeans

It appears that the first European explorers almost went out of their way not to see Queensland. The number of near sightings during the 17th century is quite remarkable. In 1605 the Portuguese explorer, **Ferdinand de Quiros**, thought he had reached Australia when he reached Vanuatu. He named the island he discovered Australia del Espiritu Santo. The following year **Luis Vaez de Torres** passed between Cape York and New Guinea without sighting northern Australia and, in 1623 **Jan Carstensz** sailed from Batavia and explored parts of the Gulf of Carpentaria. Carstensz's explorations were important. He had a number of minor battles with Aborigines and became increasingly disheartened by the harsh and barren nature of the coast. He named the coastline Carpentaria after Pieter de Carpentier, the Governor-General of the Dutch East Indies. His reports on the country discouraged further exploration.

Over a century passed and, while the Dutch regularly sailed up the coast of Western Australia their curiosity about the rest of the continent seemed limited. The last Dutch exploration ships to sail into Queensland waters were the *Rijder* and *Buis* which explored the Gulf of Carpentaria in 1756.

So poor was the knowledge of the north eastern part of Australia that William Dampier's map of the continent, which is dated 1729, includes the Gulf of Carpentaria but leaves blank a space between the northern tip and New Guinea.

EARLY SETTLEMENT OF QUEENSLAND

The first Europeans to settle in Queensland did so by accident. Captain James Cook 'settled' at Cooktown for a month in 1770 after his ship hit the Great Barrier Reef. When John Oxley explored Moreton Bay in 1823 he found it was already 'settled' by three escaped convicts – Thomas Pamphlett, Richard Parsons and John Finnegan. The convicts claimed that, while on a wood-cutting expedition, they had been swept out to sea in their small vessel which eventually washed onto Moreton Island. Local Aborigines had shown them the fresh water source.

Captain James Cook named many places along the Queensland coast. Some of the most famous are:

● **The Glasshouse Mountains:** On 17 May 1770 Cook wrote: 'These hills...very much resembles a glass house, and for this reason I called them the Glass Houses'.

● **Magnetic Island:** On 6 June 1770 Cook wrote: 'The East point I named Cape Cleveland and the West Magnetical Head or Isle as it had much the appearance of an island and the compass would not travis well when near it'.

● **Cape Tribulation:** The entries in Cook's diaries for the night of Sunday 10 June and the morning of Monday 11 June 1770 explain that he named 'the north point Cape Tribulation because here began all our troubles'. He hit the reef and had to spend a month in Cooktown repairing his ship.

Captain Cook sails up the Coast

On 20 April 1770 Captain James Cook and the crew of HM Barque *Endeavour* sighted the east coast of Australia at Point Hicks on the Victorian coast. Over the next four months Cook sailed north exploring what would become the coastlines of New South Wales and Queensland.

On 16 May Cook passed **Point Danger**, the northern headland of the Tweed River, and began to explore the coast of modern day Queensland. On 17 May he named Cape Morton (it was subsequently changed to Moreton), the northern tip of **Moreton Island** off Brisbane, and on 23 May he landed at Bustard Bay to collect fresh water. He made his way tentatively through the **Whitsunday Islands** entering the Whitsunday Passage on 4 June and reaching **Magnetic Island** on 6 June (he named the island because it seemed to affect his compass). On 11 June the *Endeavour* struck the Great Barrier Reef near **Cape Tribulation**. It limped on to the Endeavour River (the present site of Cooktown) where it remained for repairs until 6 August. On 22 August, having sailed up the entire coast of Queensland and discovered the Great Barrier Reef, Cook stood on **Possession Island** north of Cape York and claimed the whole east coast of the continent on behalf of the British Empire, naming it New South Wales.

Right: *At Townsville the old meets the new as a replica of Captain Cook's* Endeavour *moors at the city's modern marina.*
Opposite: *Now a popular tourist attraction, the Jondaryan woolshed was the largest woolshed in Queensland when it was built in 1859.*

ABORIGINAL TIME LINE

c.40,000 B.P. Aborigines move into western Queensland.
1606 Willem Jansz sails around Cape York Peninsula. Aborigines on Cape York still recall this voyage in their oral history and paintings.
1770 Captain James Cook claims possession of whole east coast of the continent using the 'Terra Nullius' argument.
1848 The hated Native Mounted Police Force established. It pits Aborigines against Aborigines.
1857 Yeemen Aborigines attack Hornet Bank station killing a number of settlers.
1861 19 Europeans killed by a party of Kairi Aborigines at Cullin-la-Ringo station near Emerald.
1895 Native Mounted Police Force disbanded.
1897 Policy established to remove 'troublesome' Aborigines to reserves.

1978 Aurukun and Mornington island Aboriginal communities established as independent local authorities.
1989 Poet and civil rights activist Oodgeroo Noonuccal becomes first woman and Aborigine to receive doctorate from Griffith University.
1990 Leslie Malezar becomes first Aborigine to head a government department.
1991 Queensland passes Aboriginal land rights legislation. Anti-discrimination legislation also introduced.
1992 High Court of Australia recognises native title and repudiates 'Terra Nullius' in Mabo case.
1994 Wik people make Native Claim on Cape York Peninsula, northern Queensland.
1996 Pauline Hanson attacks 'special treatment' for Aborigines and calls for cuts in funding.

First Settlement of Queensland

In September 1822, 34 years after Sydney Cove was founded, the British government instructed the Governor of the colony of New South Wales, Sir Thomas Brisbane, to send out exploration parties to Moreton Bay, Port Curtis and Port Bowen with a view to finding a suitable place for a new penal colony.

In November 1823 the explorer John Oxley reached the waters of Moreton Bay. Within days of his arrival he chanced upon three escaped convicts who claimed that, while on a wood-cutting expedition, they had

REDCLIFFE – THE FIRST SETTLEMENT

In July 1799 Matthew Flinders spent 15 days in Moreton Bay and landed at the current site of Redcliffe calling it Red Cliff Point. In 1823 John Oxley recommended Red Cliff Point suitable for a penal colony. On 24 September 1823 the brig *Amity* brought officials, soldiers, their wives and children, and 29 convicts to Redcliffe. The first European babies born in Queensland arrived in September and November 1824.

Three weeks after the establishment of the settlement two convicts and a soldier were speared to death by local Aborigines and this, plus the prevalence of fever and poor anchorage facilities, led the settlement to be moved to the banks of the Brisbane River.

Above: *The gentle arc of the Brisbane River, the location for Queensland's capital, was the site of a convict settlement in 1825.*

THE EXPLORATION OF INLAND QUEENSLAND

1844–45 Ludwig Leichhardt travelled to Cape York, across the Gulf of Carpentaria to Port Essington in the Northern Territory.
1846 Sir Thomas Mitchell travelled north through Central Queensland.
1847–48 E.B. Kennedy discovered the Barcoo River and Cooper Creek, and explored the coast from Rockingham Bay to Cape York.
1858 A.C. Gregory travelled from Adelaide, up Cooper Creek and into Queensland.
1864–65 The Jardine Brothers explored from Rockhampton to Bowen.

been swept out to sea. The convicts showed Oxley the local supply of fresh water and he named it the Brisbane River after the governor.

Oxley returned to Sydney Town with news of the discovery. The next year Governor Brisbane sent the explorer back to Moreton Bay accompanied by 29 convicts, 14 soldiers, the botanist Allan Cunningham, a surgeon and storekeeper named Walter Scott, and the settlement's first military commandant, Lieutenant Henry Miller.

Before the small sailing ship *Amity* left Sydney Cove, Brisbane told Oxley: 'The Amity is placed under orders for the purpose of crowning your late discovery of a large river flowing into Moreton Bay with the formation of a new settlement in its vicinity. The spot which you select must contain three hundred acres of land, and be in the neighbourhood of fresh water. It should lay in the direct course to the mouth of the river, be easily seen from the offing of ready access. To difficulty of attack by the natives, it ought to join difficulty of escape for the convicts.'

The first settlement was at Redcliffe on Moreton Bay. Three months later the site was moved to North Quay on the Brisbane River.

Exploration of Queensland

The first explorer to travel by land into the area was **John Oxley** who, in 1823, discovered the Tweed River and recommended Moreton Bay as suitable for a penal colony.

The government prevented free settlers entering the area around the colony until 1842 when Governor Gipps declared that 'all settlers and other free persons shall be at liberty to proceed to the **Darling Downs** in like manner as to any other part of the Colony'.

Almost immediately settlers moved into the coastal area and crops of sugar cane were grown while sheep, dairy and beef cattle were raised in the hinterland. The graziers, with their substantial production of wool, hides and tallow, forced the opening up of a number of ports on the coast.

Although the Darling Downs had been explored as early as the 1820s (Allan Cunningham passed through the area in 1823) it wasn't until the government allowed squatters and pastoralists to move onto the rich and fertile plains that the area was settled.

By 1844 Jimbour Station was the furthest outpost of European settlement. Beyond it lay an unexplored wilderness. The explorer **Ludwig Leichhardt** left Jimbour on 1 October and for the next 15 months travelled 5000km (3000 miles) into western Queensland and the north east of Northern Territory arriving exhausted at Port Essington on 17 December 1845. As a result of Leichhardt's glowing reports on the land beyond Jimbour there was a push for settlement of this central western region.

Beyond here lay the vast, flat near-desert of the Gulf country and the Great Artesian Basin which was first explored by **Burke and Wills** in 1860 who travelled from Melbourne to the Gulf of Carpentaria. They both died.

> ### BURKE AND WILLS
>
> The ill-fated Burke and Wills expedition started from Menindee in western New South Wales, crossed into south-western Queensland then, after moving through the southern section of the Northern Territory, moved north through Queensland towards the Gulf of Carpentaria. Both Burke and Wills perished although it is known that the local Aborigines tried to feed them. They discovered nothing, but the explorers who came searching for them – notably Howitt, Landsborough, McKinlay and Walker – all opened up the rich pasture lands of north-western Queensland.

Below: *When Burke and Wills reached the Gulf of Carpentaria in 1861 they had travelled for weeks through the dry, harsh desert landscape of western Queensland.*

THE QUEENSLAND GERRYMANDER

The Queensland government changed only three times between 1915 and 1995 because a gerrymander favoured the party in power at elections. The Australian Labor Party won in 1915 and remained until 1957 when it lost power because of a split within the party. The Liberal–Country coalition came to power in 1957 and under Premier Johannes Bjelke-Petersen, premier from 1968, they remained until the ALP were returned in 1989. Eliminating the gerrymander meant changes of govern-ment were more likely. In February 1996, due to a by-election, not a state election, the balance of power was delivered to an Independent member who supported the Liberal–National Party coalition. The ALP again lost power.

The subsequent expeditions of **Frederick Walker**, **William Landsborough** and **John McKinlay** scoured the area for the ill-fated Burke and Wills and in the process discovered both the pastoral and mining potential of the Gulf.

The next major development occurred when gold was discovered in Gympie, along the Palmer River and at various points on the Atherton Tablelands, in the 1860s and 1870s.

The towns appearing on the coast were all built for one reason: to provide port access. Townsville, Cardwell, Port Douglas, Cairns and Cooktown all started life as ports from which gold could be shipped out.

The construction of the ports was no great challenge, it was finding routes from the tablelands down the steep escarpment. The early pioneer trail blazers – men like **Christie Palmerston** and **John Atherton** – were confronted with sheer cliffs, dense rainforest and fierce local Aborigines.

John Atherton, after whom the tablelands are named, first overlanded cattle to the Herberton fields when he realised that the miners needed to be fed.

Right: *Under the 'Tree of Knowledge' at Barcaldine striking shearers met. It was here that the infant Australian Labor Party was formed in 1891.*

Left: *First occupied in 1868, and finally completed in 1889, Brisbane's Parliament House is characterised by solid colonnades which keep the building cool in summer.*

GOVERNMENT AND ECONOMY

On 10 December 1859 Queensland became a separate colony. At the time the population was 23,520. The first Governor was **Sir George Bowen**. The colony grew rapidly as settlers, recognising the economic potential of the state, settled both the coast and the inland areas.

Almost immediately the governor had to deal with problems of land management. The 'squatters' (people who literally arrived in an area and without approval from the government, staked the land and started farming) claimed they were helping the infant colony and demanded the government turn their 'squatting' into permanent tenure. The government refused arguing that it wanted more intensive land use and wanted to maintain control over crown land. The battle raged through the 1860s to the 1880s. During this time no fewer than 22 major **Land Act bills** passed through the Queensland Parliament. It is hardly surprising that the end result pleased neither the government nor the squatters.

By the 1880s there was a perception that the graziers were ruling the state. This led, in 1891 in the tiny western Queensland township of **Barcaldine**, to the formation of the **Australian Labor Party** – one of the first trade union based worker's parties formed anywhere in the world.

QUEENSLAND – GROWTH IN THE 1980s

Australia experienced two major recessions in the 1980s (1983 and 1989). During both, large numbers of people moved to Queensland believing the state had better opportunities. This perception was partly the result of the state's booming tourism industry, partly due to many people from Victoria and NSW moving north to retire, and partly because Queensland Premier, Johannes Bjelke-Petersen, persuaded the rest of Australia that Queensland was a state of opportunity. These changes were reflected in the state's population increase by 25.4 per cent in 1983–93 and the increase from 9.8 per cent to 11.1 per cent of population over 65 years of age.

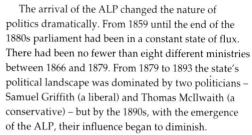

ABORIGINAL RESISTANCE

Queensland's Aborigines resisted the advance of European civilisation. In 1857 at Hornet Bank station a group of over 100 Aborigines attacked white settlers killing 12 of the 15 people living on the property. In 1861 at the nearby Cullin-la-Ringo station 19 whites were killed by a party of Kairi Aborigines. Similarly the explorer Edmund Kennedy was killed by Aborigines while trying to travel from Rockingham to Cape York, and on Fraser Island Captain James Fraser and his crew were enslaved by the local Aborigines.

The arrival of the ALP changed the nature of politics dramatically. From 1859 until the end of the 1880s parliament had been in a constant state of flux. There had been no fewer than eight different ministries between 1866 and 1879. From 1879 to 1893 the state's political landscape was dominated by two politicians – Samuel Griffith (a liberal) and Thomas McIlwaith (a conservative) – but by the 1890s, with the emergence of the ALP, their influence began to diminish.

Queensland joined the Commonwealth of Australia in 1901. By 1915 the Australian Labor Party were in power in the state. This was the beginning of the longest period of continuous government in Australian history. They remained in power until 1957. So powerful was the Australian Labor Party that in 1922 they managed to abolish the **Legislative Council** (the State's upper house – roughly equivalent to the British House of Lords).

Today Queensland is the only state in Australia without a Legislative Council.

A split within the Australian Labor Party resulted in a victory for a coalition of conservative parties (the Liberal and Country parties) which remained in power from 1957 until 1989. From 1968 the state was ruled by **Sir Johannes Bjelke-Petersen**, a larger-than-life character who claimed that he was doing what all Queenslanders wanted him to do. Bjelke-Petersen encouraged overseas tourism and overseas development of coastal resorts, actively propagated the idea that Queensland was a state of unlimited opportunity, and ruled the state in a highly idiosyncratic way.

THE PEOPLE
The First Inhabitants

It is likely that the first Aborigines arrived in north Queensland around 45,000 years ago. They were hunters and gatherers who moved slowly across from the coast of the Northern Territory where they had arrived probably 10,000 years earlier. There is evidence that they settled throughout the state: numerous middens (mounds of discarded shells) exist along the coast and there are a number of important inland sites where groups settled in well-protected caves. There is considerable evidence that the Aborigines of north Queensland traded with Aborigines across the northern half of the continent and shared many aspects of their culture.

Findings in Cape York suggest the Aboriginal relationship to the land remained relatively unchanged for thousands of years and was only affected by changes in sea level and major climatic changes. Thus Queensland Aborigines lived on a mixture of yams, nuts, lady apple and bandicoots, snakes, possums and small kangaroos known as bettongs. The people on the coast were more dependent on molluscs gathered from the rock platforms and fish caught in the shallows.

It is an interesting aspect of Queensland Aborigines that they fought tenaciously to protect their land. There are a number of incidents where early settlers and explorers were attacked and, on the Central Highlands, there are still farm houses with gun emplacements to protect against possible attacks.

Above: *Sugar cane has been vital for the economy of north Queensland since it was first grown in 1862. The narrow railway lines and sugar mills are a distinctive part of the landscape.*

Opposite: *There are many interesting Aboriginal cultural centres throughout Queensland. The most notable are Kalkadoon at Mt Isa (pictured here) and those at Cairns and Rockhampton.*

WHERE QUEENSLANDERS LIVED IN 1999		
Brisbane and Moreton Bay	2,277,342	65%
Wide Bay-Burnett	232,987	6.6%
Darling Downs	201,446	5.7%
South West	25,711	0.7%
Fitzroy	181,202	5.1%
Central West	12,255	0.3%
Mackay	125,977	3.6%
Northern	197,302	5.6%
Far North	222,451	6.3%
North West	35,682	1.1%

Above: *Queensland is a culturally diverse society. These dancers, the children of eastern European settlers, entertain workers at Queen Street Mall at lunchtime.*

Early Settlers

There were three major reasons why people settled in Queensland in the 19th century – grazing, sugar cane and gold.

The first settlers were **graziers** and **farmers** who, after 1842, moved north to graze sheep and cattle on the rich pasture lands. By the 1840s they had settled the Darling Downs and the areas to the west of Brisbane. By the 1850s they were further north and by the 1860s and 1870s the process was largely complete. The settlement varied from marginal lands in western Queensland to tropical dairy farming on the Atherton Tablelands.

About the same time as settlers were moving herds of sheep and cattle into the inland, other settlers realised the **sugar cane** potential of the rich coastal lands. They quickly established sugar fields and sought cheap labour from the South Pacific islands.

The third major push started with the discovery of gold at **Gympie** in 1867. The major gold discoveries in Victoria and New South Wales had occurred by this time and the miners and prospectors were looking for new fields. From 1867 until the late 1880s a series of major discoveries were made. Each new discovery brought large numbers of miners to fields which stretched from Gympie north to the Atherton Tablelands and the famous Palmer River goldfields to the west of Cooktown.

The New Australians

Today Queensland, like the rest of Australia, is a genuinely multicultural society with substantial populations of Chinese, Italians, Vietnamese and South Pacific Islanders. This racial mixture has not been without its problems. The infamous **'White Australia' policy** (never a formal policy but an informal, unstated immigration arrangement) grew out of attempts to prevent the use of immigrant labour on the sugar plantations and to restrict the immigration of Chinese onto the north Queensland gold fields.

The most interesting aspects of Queensland's multicultural society are the stories of the South Pacific Islanders and Italians who arrived to work on the sugar plantations.

The South Pacific Islanders

Over 61,000 Pacific Islanders arrived to work on the Queensland canefields between 1863–1904. They were known as 'kanakas' – indentured labourers who worked in virtual slavery. The first 67 'kanakas' arrived from the New Hebrides and Loyalty islands aboard the 100-ton schooner, *Don Juan*, on 15 August 1863. They were to be employed by Robert Towns on his 1620ha (4000 acre) cotton plantation on the Logan River. The term applied to this process of virtual slavery was 'blackbirding'.

On 26 April 1867 Ross Lewin, who was to become one of the most successful blackbirders, advertised that he could provide the 'best and most serviceable natives to be had in the islands at £7 a head'.

The term of 'indenture' was three years and, while the 'kanakas' were not slaves, they had few freedoms and little concept of the work and conditions they were agreeing to.

The 'kanakas' were vital to the development of the state's sugar industry. It was a sad truth that sugar prices around the world were, without exception, the result of the use of cheap labour.

The Immigration Act passed by the new federal government in 1901 authorised the deportation of any 'kanakas' found in Australia after 1906. The only exceptions were those who had lived in Australia for 20 years or more, had married in Australia or owned property. About 3600 'kanakas' were returned to their islands at the end of 1906.

KANAKAS – TIME LINE

1847 Benjamin Boyd brings South Pacific islanders to NSW to work on his sheep stations.
1863 First 'kanakas' arrive from the New Hebrides and Loyalty islands aboard *Don Juan* to work on cotton plantation on the Logan River.
1867 Ross Lewin advertises: 'best and most serviceable natives to be had in the islands at £7 a head'.
1884 Pacific Island Labourers Act was amended so that 'kanakas' could only work in the sugar industry.
1901 Federal Government Immigration Act authorises the deportation of 'kanakas' found in Australia after 1906.
1906 Final repatriation. 61,160 Pacific Islanders had arrived to work on the Queensland cane fields between 1863–1904.

Below: *The 'kanakas' were instrumental in the development of the sugar industry. Today the cane is still burnt before cutting.*

WHO USES CULTURE

A survey in Queensland in 1991 revealed the following levels of usage of the state's cultural facilities over a 12-month period:

Library	34.5%
Art Gallery	23.4%
Museum	27.1%
Popular Music Concert	29.3%
Dance Performance	11%
Musical Theatre	20.2%
Other Theatrical Performance	17.1%
Classical music Concerts	6.9%

The Italians

Sugar plantation owners began to look elsewhere for people prepared to do the backbreaking job of cutting cane. As a result a substantial number of Italians came to Australia in the 1890s to work on the Queensland sugar cane fields.

Like most European countries, Italy was unstable and near-ruin during the years between World War I and II. This led to large-scale emigration. Australia's 1921 census revealed that there were over 8000 Italians living here, and by 1933 this figure had grown to 26,500. Already the Italians had become Australia's largest immigrant group after the British and the Irish.

In Queensland local canefield workers protested their jobs were being endangered by Italian emigrants, but it is probably more correct to recognise that the canefields were sustained by Italian workers. The cemetery near Innisfail has a distinctive section of imposing Italian family mausoleums.

Queensland's Cultural Life

While Queensland has the usual array of theatres, art galleries, symphony orchestras, museums and centres of cultural excellence, it is essentially an outdoor society. It has more claims than most modern western societies to being a genuine working people's paradise: the beaches are good, the food is fresh and plentiful, the days of sunshine are long and clear, the society is open and casual. At the heart of Queensland's culture lies a healthy love of sunshine and recreation.

Having said that, it is worth noting that Queensland has made a vital contribution to the

Below: *A popular tourist attraction for visitors to Kuranda, the Tjapukai Dance Theatre celebrates north Queensland's Aboriginal culture.*

cultural life of Australia. The life of the early settlers, particularly those in outback Queensland, was an inspiration to Australia's greatest bush balladeers – A. B. 'Banjo' Paterson and Henry Lawson. It was near Winton that Paterson first penned the famous bush ballad 'Waltzing Matilda', and Lawson, a great short story writer, found his inspiration in the ordinary lives of the people who worked on the vast outback sheep properties.

For many years Australians from the southern states looked upon Queensland as the 'Deep North' and scoffed at the thought that the state may have a healthy cultural life. In recent times this has changed as major cultural centres have been built (the South Bank Cultural Centre in Brisbane is as fine a collection of theatres, galleries, libraries and museums as exists anywhere in Australia) and local culture, particularly Aboriginal culture, has been actively encouraged.

The Tjapukai Aboriginal Cultural Park at Cairns in North Queensland have been recognised as one of the finest Aboriginal dance companies in the land. They have become so successful that they created one of the first indigenous theme parks in the world with the Tjapukai Cultural Complex offering a unique insight into indigenous culture. They also encourage other Aboriginal communities to present their culture to the world.

On the Gold Coast the construction of Warner Bros Movie World, with an associated collection of state-of-the-art film studios, has attracted international film production teams (and ancillary workers) to the area.

Queensland has some excellent regional facilities. The major coastal cities – particularly Rockhampton, Townsville and Cairns – are well provided with art galleries and museums. Equally a variety of entertainments ranging from international productions to local musicals, pop music concerts, orchestras and ballet troupes, regularly tour the state.

Above: *Street theatre ranging from fire eaters to jugglers and buskers is common at malls, tourist locations and cultural centres.*

ABORIGINAL CULTURE

Aboriginal culture is as sophisticated as its technology is simple. Complex ceremonies fusing song, dance, body painting, religion and history express the lore of the Dreamtime; the eternal presence, the activities and the unpredictable influence of the beings who were the creators of all creatures and things, and the laws relating to interaction with each other and the land. They also tell where to hunt, the location of food and water, and ideal marriage partners.

2
Brisbane

In his book *Portrait of Brisbane* Bill Scott wrote: 'Brisbane is a lazy town with its sleeves rolled up, casually sprawling across its thirty-seven hills. The hills are patterned with paling fences, mango trees, high-stepping weather-board houses, and a tangle of overhead wires like the web of a demented spider.'

Today this description of Brisbane is out-of-date but the central thrust – that it is a subtropical city which thrives on informality – still captures the spirit of the city. While it may seem to the new arrival just another modern city of freeways and skyscrapers, it does have a distinct tropical feel and this produces a fascinating mixture of regionalism and informality. It is, in a real sense, a very large and sophisticated country town.

Brisbane varies significantly from all other Australian state capitals. Firstly it is a subtropical city with an oppressive summer temperature range that demands office buildings be airconditioned and that outside workers protect themselves against the debilitating effects of the subtropical sun.

· Secondly, it is not the only major centre in the state. Whereas other states radiate out from their capital, Queensland, because of its size and its decentralization, can claim Brisbane as its centre of government while acknowledging the regional importance of cities like Townsville and Rockhampton.

Thirdly, it is the capital of the country's fastest growing state and, as such, it has changed from a large country town to a modern financial centre.

DON'T MISS

*** Botanic Gardens:
a beautiful retreat beside the Brisbane River and a rich display of tropical plants.
** South Bank Cultural Centre: an ideal walk along the banks of the Brisbane as well as an interesting museum, library and range of theatres.
** Stradbroke Island:
an easy ferry trip to an island full of delights.
** Mt Coot-tha Botanic Gardens: superb tropical gardens in a pleasant suburban setting.

Opposite: *Brisbane is an attractive modern city located on the banks of the Brisbane River.*

Opposite above: *Old Government House was built in 1862. A Classical Revival building built of porphyry and sandstone, it remained the Governor's official residence until 1910.*

HISTORIC BRISBANE

Brisbane started life as a penal colony. In 1822 the Governor of New South Wales, Sir Thomas Brisbane, sent a party led by the explorer John Oxley to inspect sites at Moreton Bay, Port Curtis and Port Bowen to evaluate their suitability as penal colonies.

Oxley arrived at Moreton Bay in November 1823 and was immediately impressed with its good location and substantial supply of fresh water. The following year, on the basis of this recommendation, Brisbane

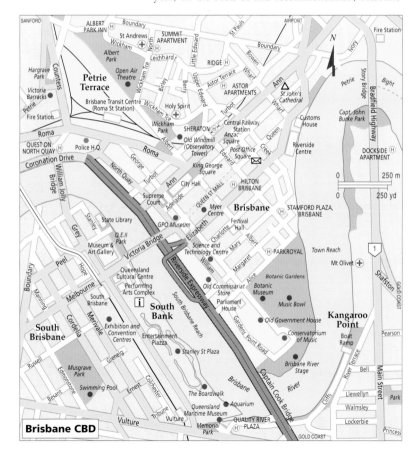

Brisbane CBD

sent Oxley, 29 convicts, 14 soldiers, the botanist Allan Cunningham, a surgeon and storekeeper named Walter Scott, and the settlement's first military commandant, Lieutenant Henry Miller, to establish a settlement at the modern day site of Redcliffe.

The site was short-lived. Three months later they moved to North Quay on the Brisbane River. When Chief Justice Forbes arrived in December 1824 it was decided that the colony should be called 'Edinglassie' but this was rejected for Brisbane in recognition of the Governor's role in the founding of the colony.

Brisbane did not grow until 1842 when the Moreton Bay area was opened to free settlers. The period up to the 1850s was difficult as the city struggled to establish its independence from Sydney. When Queensland became an independent colony in 1859 the city grew rapidly. In 1861 the population was 6051. Thirty years later it was 101,554. It officially became a city in 1902. During World War II it became a vital military position and over two million allied troops used it as their headquarters and as a centre for rest and recreation. Since the war the city has continued to grow. The population of Greater Brisbane passed two million in the early 1990s.

Below: *The Old Windmill is located in Wickham Terrace and dates back to 1828.*

BRISBANE'S HISTORIC BUILDINGS

Brisbane has a tradition of newness and consequently it has relatively few genuinely old public buildings of importance. This can partly be explained by the city's long history of timber construction and the fact that in 1864 a fire destroyed many of the city's finest early buildings. However, the remaining old buildings are gracious and impressive.

The Old Commissariat Store ***

The most interesting buildings in the city include **The Old Windmill** sometimes known as Observatory Tower and the **The Old Commissariat Store** at 111 William Street which was built by convicts when Brisbane was a closed penal colony. It is now the headquarters of the Royal Historical Society of Queensland. Reputed to be the state's first stone building, it was constructed with walls which ranged in thickness from 60cm (2ft) to 1.2m (4ft). The first building was completed in 1829 as a two-storey structure but over the period 1886–1926 it was expanded to three storeys.

Customs House **

With its solid Corinthian columns and its greenish copper dome the **Customs House** stands beside the Brisbane River like a great Victorian matriarch. Its position and prominence ensure that it is one of Brisbane's most impressive landmarks. It was built by John Petrie between 1886 and 1889 and features twin pediments with heraldic shields and the words 'Advance Australia', a noble thought although, at the time of construction, there was no 'Australia'.

St John's Cathedral **

This Gothic church, at 417 Ann Street, is built in brick and Brisbane porphyry stone. Building was started in 1901 and, even today, the western section remains unfinished. New bays were completed in 1968 and a model of how the cathedral will eventually look is located in the church.

General Post Office **

At 261 Queen Street, the **General Post Office** is on the site of the city's original female convict barracks. On the first floor is the **GPO Museum** (open 10:00–15:00 on Tuesday, Wednesday and Thursday) which exhibits a fascinating range of old postal, radio and telegraphic equipment including morse code equipment and early telephones.

Old Government House **

Located between the Queensland Institute of Technology and the Brisbane River, old **Government House** was built in 1862 when the population of Brisbane was a mere 6000. A Classical Revival building it was designed by Charles Tiffin, built of porphyry and sandstone, and constructed between 1860–62. It remained the Governor's official residence until 1910 after which it was used as the first building of the University of Queensland. It is currently used as the offices for the **National Trust of Queensland**. Apart from a range of publications the National Trust also have a comprehensive listing of churches, old buildings, historic sites and landmarks throughout Brisbane.

Parliament House **

Nearby is the state's **Parliament House**. Immediately after Queensland was declared a separate colony in 1859, Brisbane saw the large and gracious Parliament House building rising on the hill above the Botanic Gardens. The colonial architect, Charles Tiffin, was commissioned to build Parliament House after he won a national competition with his unusual imitation of the French Renaissance style. The building was started in 1865, first occupied in 1868, and completed in 1889. It is characterised by colonnades which keep the building cool in summer, some magnificent timber work executed in Queensland timbers, and a gracious interior.

Below: *Brisbane's General Post Office is one of the city's central meeting places. Located at 261 Queen Street, it is built on the site of the city's first female convict barracks.*

Above: *Brisbane held an Expo in 1988 and the buildings, located on the south bank of the Brisbane River, have been converted into a cultural and convention centre.*
Opposite *The shopping heart of Brisbane is the Queen Street Mall with its wide range of specialist shops and impressive department stores like the Myer Centre.*

Queensland Cultural Centre ***

Just over the Victoria Bridge from the city's central business district is the Southbank which includes the **Queensland Cultural Centre**, one of the country's finest cultural complexes. Set on the banks of the Brisbane River it includes the John Oxley Library, the Queensland Museum (with two million items including the tiny 'Avian Cirrus' aeroplane in which Bert Hinkler made the first solo flight from England to Australia in 1928), many restaurants, and the Performing Arts Complex – Lyric Theatre, Concert Hall and Cremorne Studio Theatre. Apart from offering visitors an excellent opportunity to wander along the banks of the Brisbane River, the complex also hosts overseas performers as well as the best local productions of musicals and plays.

City Hall Art Gallery **

One of Brisbane's most historic landmarks is the **City Hall Art Gallery and Museum** complex which combines King George Square, the Brisbane Administration Centre and the City Plaza Shopping Centre. The City Hall Art Gallery and Museum were opened by Queen Elizabeth II in 1977 and contain displays of paintings, ceramics and photographs. The clock tower, rising 91m (300ft) above the City Plaza, provides panoramic views of the city.

City Hall *

The **City Hall** is an interesting example of English neo-classical architecture in a modern building of Queensland brown-tinted freestone, marble, sandstone and timbers. The scale is impressive and full of old world charm. The main foyer inside King George Square uses ornate high vaulted ceilings, floor mosaics, and crafted timber and plasterwork to great effect. There is also a huge 16m (52ft) sculpture depicting Queensland protecting her citizens.

Queensland Maritime Museum ★★★

The **Queensland Maritime Museum** is located on the river at the end of Dock Street. It features an interesting display of charts, model ships, engines and memorabilia, combined with 'on the water' displays of a World War II frigate and an old steam tug.

Victoria Barracks ★★

Located in Petrie Terrace the old **Victoria Barracks** were built between 1864–74 to a design which had been drawn up by the War Office in London. Today the barracks are a military museum housing weapons, old uniforms, photographs and memorabilia.

SHOPPING IN BRISBANE

Visitors to Brisbane will find that the city has a wide variety of shops ranging from the usual array of duty free shops selling gifts, perfumes, photographic and electronic equipment, to specialist gift shops selling interesting pieces of Australiana, and department stores where there is a wide range of Australian and overseas goods. There is no bargaining in Australian shops and, as a general principle, there will be a slight mark up in large arcades because of the high rental costs.

People looking for quality Australian gifts should visit the **M.E. Humfress and Co** at 56 Tower Street, Ascot, tel: (07) 3262-6685. They offer a wide range of gifts including kangaroo fur, leather goods and genuine sheepskin products. Equally interesting, although more specialised, are the **National Trust Gift Shop** at 40 George Street (tel: (07) 3221-1887) which offers a range of tasteful National Trust gifts as well as hand-crafted Australian products including prints, pictures, books and stationery.

> **GOOD SHOPPING**
>
> The centre of Brisbane's shopping is the Queen Street Mall, two city blocks which have been closed off to vehicles. Places worth visiting include:
> - **Broadway on the Mall:** Queen Street Mall.
> - **The Wintergarden:** Queen Street Mall.
> - **The Myer Centre:** Queen Street Mall.
> - **Brisbane Arcade:** between Queen and Adelaide Streets.
> - **Rowes Arcade:** Edward Street.

Queensland has an active and successful gem mining industry and Brisbane is a good place to find opals and other interesting gemstones. **The Rock Shop** at 193 Adelaide Street (tel: (07) 3221-0981) has been in business for over a quarter of a century.

Visitors looking to simply explore the city's variety of shops should head toward the city's major shopping arcades which include the **T&G Arcade** on the corner of Queen and Albert streets, the **Wintergarden on the Mall** on the Queen Street Mall, **Rowes Arcade** on Edward Street, the **Myer Centre** at the top of the Queen Street Mall and the **City Plaza Shopping Centre** which is located behind the City Hall with access from George, Ann, and Adelaide streets. All these centres offer a wide range of specialist shops and department stores, such as Myers who are regarded as purveyors of quality goods at reasonable prices.

THE BRISBANE RIVER

A simple pleasure, and one of the best ways to appreciate the beauty of the city's location on the Brisbane River, is to walk across the numerous bridges which cross the river.

Below: *The Story Bridge is one of seven that cross the Brisbane River allowing easy access to the central business district.*

Victoria Bridge

The **Victoria Bridge** affords excellent views back towards the city and takes the pedestrian to the South Bank complex. Continue either north or south along the river bank as both provide attractive vantage points to view the city. Although it is not the oldest bridge across the Brisbane River (the William Jolly Bridge can claim that distinction), the Victoria Bridge is the third bridge to be built on a site which was the earliest European crossing point. A pylon from the second bridge (1897) has been retained as a monument

and is now listed on the National Estate. On the pylon is a plaque to a Greek boy who was killed during World War I victory celebrations in 1918.

Story Bridge *

The most spectacular vantage point is from **Story Bridge** which arches high from Captain John Burke Park. It is not an easy walk but the views of the city skyline, with the ferries crossing the river further upstream, is an excellent orientation and a simple way to understand the beauty of the city. The Story Bridge's claim to fame lies in the poor bedrock of Brisbane. In order to construct the Story Bridge it was necessary to dig down 40.2m (131ft) to establish a firm foundation, one of the deepest foundations in the world.

Above: *On the banks of the Brisbane River the Botanic Gardens offer cool relief from the bustle of the city centre.*

Botanic Gardens **

The city **Botanic Gardens** cover over 20ha (50 acres) of land. Beautifully located on the banks of the Brisbane River and spreading over the gentle slopes and undulations below Parliament House and the Old Government House, the gardens are a peaceful respite from the bustle of the Central Business District.

The Botanic Gardens date back to the earliest years of European settlement. Long before 1855, when they were formally laid out by Walter Hill the first gardens director, the area had been used as a vegetable garden.

Hill planted rows of bunya pines and introduced plants like the poinciana and jacaranda. He also built a fountain in 1867 and planted a row of weeping figs.

Brisbane's subtropical climate, combined with the rich soils of the river bank, ensures a permanent display of spectacular colours and heady fragrances of frangipanis, orchids, oleanders, flame trees, bougainvilleas and jacarandas. A walk through the gardens, particularly a walk along the river bank, is a must for every visitor to the city. On a hot summer day there is a sense of tranquillity and coolness about the gardens.

> ### CITY OF TROPICAL PARKS
>
> Brisbane's warm, moist climate ensures that the city's 200 parks and gardens are its greatest attraction. The displays of orchids, flame trees, bougainvilleas, frangipanis, oleanders and jacarandas make the City Botanic Gardens so impressive. The park on the South Bank also offers excellent views of the city. Be sure to see the dome-shaped indoor display at Mount Coot-tha Reserve which houses a virtual tropical rainforest. Mt Coot-tha also has a Japanese Garden, a herb garden and some Australian rain forest.

Brisbane at a Glance

BEST TIMES TO VISIT

Queensland divides its seasons into 'wet and dry'. The best time to visit is **June** to **September** (dry). This is officially winter, however, the days are warm and the nights cool and pleasant. In summertime the city's weather can be hot and oppressive.

GETTING THERE

The Brisbane international and domestic airports are close to each other and are about 12km (8 miles) north east of the city centre. **Coachtrains** runs a shuttle bus from both terminals to the Transit Centre in the city every half hour from 05:00 to 23:00. **Taxis** are available at both airports as are the major car rental firms.

The Transit Centre in Roma Street is the main terminus and booking point for all long-distance trains and buses. Brisbane is well serviced by both trains and buses. The XPT train from Sydney takes 14 hours and runs daily.

The major bus companies all travel to and from other state capital cities to Brisbane.

GETTING AROUND

The bus service in Brisbane is efficient and easy to use. Bus stops in the city centre are colour coded for convenience. The city circle bus does a clockwise loop every

five minutes. The City train network has seven lines running to the suburbs. All trains go through the Transit Centre in Roma Street. Car rental firms are well represented with all the major companies as well as many smaller rental agencies. The Brisbane River flows through the centre of the city and there are regular ferries and cruise ships.

WHERE TO STAY

Brisbane is not only a tourist destination but the capital of Queensland. It has a dynamic and busy city centre. Accommodation ranges from luxury five-star, serviced apartments to modestly priced bed and breakfast.

The Heritage Hotel, Cnr Margaret and Edwards streets, tel: (07) 3221-1999, fax: 3221-6895, or toll free: 1800 773 700. Central, luxurious hotel near the waterside and Botanic Gardens.

Hilton Brisbane, Elizabeth Street, tel: (07) 3234-2000, fax: 3221-6895. The Hilton's well-established reputation for excellent service and style is evident throughout.

The Abbey Plaza Hotel, Roma Street, tel: (07) 3236-1444, fax: 3236-1134, or toll free: 1800 777 911. Centrally located, quality accommodation with all the facilities.

Quest on North Quay, tel: (07) 3236-1440, fax: 3236-

1582, or toll free: 1800 777 694. North Quay, hotel in the heart of the city overlooking the Brisbane River, some suites with cooking facilities.

BUDGET

Bellevue Hotel, George Street, tel: (07) 3221-6044, fax: 3221-7474. Centrally located, well-priced hotel, with all the facilities of a more expensive hotel.

Centra Brisbane, Roma Street, tel: (07) 3238-2222, fax: 3238-2288. Good clean accommodation, excellent facilities, well located.

Mercure Hotel Brisbane, North Quay, tel: (07) 3236-3300, fax: 3236-1035. Overlooks the Brisbane River and Southbank parklands, central location.

The Astor Apartments, 35 Astor Terrace, tel: (07) 3839-9022, fax: 3229-5553. Reasonable, fully serviced apartments offering high quality modern conveniences.

WHERE TO EAT

Brisbane has a large range of restaurants catering to all tastes. Queensland is famous for its seafood – mud crab, Moreton Bay bugs and barramundi. Tender beef and wonderful tropical fruits are common. For a wide range of suggestions check **This Week in Brisbane** and also the magazine, **Dining Out**.

Brisbane at a Glance

Breakfast Creek Wharf Restaurant, Newstead, tel: (07) 3253-3451. An Exceptional seafood restaurant where only the freshest fish is served.

Augustine's on George, 40 George St, tel: (07) 3229-0014. Quality restaurant, centrally located.

Michael's Riverside Restaurant, Riverside Centre, tel: (07) 3832-5522. River views are an added attraction at this restaurant specialising in Italian and traditional cuisine.

Mount Coot-tha Summit Restaurant, Mount Coot-tha, tel: (07) 3369-9922. A superb view over the city and out to Moreton Bay from this mountain-top restaurant.

Pier Nine, cnr Creek and Eagle streets, tel: (07) 3229-2194. Fresh fish cooked with flair, lovely river views.

Siggi's at the Heritage, cnr Edward and Margaret streets, tel: (07) 3221-1999. Part of the Heritage Hotel group, elegant old-world charm, European cooking at its best.

Brisbane Paddlewheeler, tel: (07) 3219-6922. It departs from No. 1 Pier North Quay. This old world paddlewheeler cruises the Brisbane River both day and night.

Boomerang Tours, tel: (07) 3221-2299. Departs from the Travel Centre, has a wide variety of coach tours.

Coachtrans Day Tour, Transit Centre, Roma Street, tel: (07) 3236-4165. An inexpensive and enjoyable way to discover Brisbane.

Mirimar Cruises, Queens Wharf Road, North Quay, tel: (07) 3221-0300. Daily trips to Koala Sanctuary.

4WD Wilderness Tours, tel: (07) 5476-7439, or toll free: 1800 800 399. Get off the beaten track and explore the hinterland in four-wheel drives.

Bay Dolphin Sailing Tours, tel: (07) 3207-9620, mobile: 0427 641 669. Discover Morton Bay and enjoy an on-board lunch with friendly staff.

Koala Tours, tel: (07) 3229 7055. Runs a tour to the Lone Pine Koala Sanctuary. This is one of Australia's best known animal sanctuaries.

Pursuit Tours, tel: (07) 3398-7709. Visit historic Street Helena Island, an early penal colony; they also offer dive and charter trips.

Balloons over Brisbane, tel: (07) 3844-6671, fax: 3844-8228. Offers aarly morning hot air ballooning over Brisbane city, Beenleigh and Gatton, wonderful way to see the beauty of Queensland. There is a champagne breakfast on landing, flights daily.

Royal Automobile Club of Queensland, tel: (07) 3361-2444. Edward Street: offers a comprehensive series of road maps and helpful information for the traveller.

Environmental Protection Agency, tel: (07) 3227-7111. A must for explorers and bush walkers located on Ann Street, open Monday to Friday during business hours.

Holiday Services Tours and Cruises, tel: (07) 3236-1054. Located at the Transit Centre, information on Brisbane and the surrounding areas.

The Queensland Travel Centre, 243 Edward Street, tel: (07) 3221-6111. It is primarily a booking office for tours and excursions.

TOWN NAME	J	F	M	A	M	J	J	A	S	O	N	D
AVERAGE TEMP. °C	25	25	24	21	19	16	15	16	18	21	23	24
AVERAGE TEMP. °F	77	77	75	71	66	61	59	61	65	69	73	76
HOURS OF SUN DAILY	8	7	7	7	6	7	7	8	9	8	8	9
RAINFALL mm	161	177	144	93	86	73	65	43	33	95	95	124
RAINFALL ins.	6	7	6	4	3	3	3	2	1	4	4	5
DAYS OF RAINFALL	13	14	14	11	10	7	7	7	7	10	10	11

3
Around Brisbane

Like most modern cities, the centre is less interesting than the attractions which surround the city. If you are interested in historic buildings and shopping, the city centre is ideal. If you want to explore the Australian bush, visit beaches and nearby islands and glimpse rural Queensland, it is vital to explore beyond the suburban limits.

Surrounding Brisbane are nearly 200 lavish parks and well-kept reserves. A keen visitor can take a journey to Mount Nebo and visit a number of these stunning parks.

To the west lie the elegant cities of Ipswich and Toowoomba. Ipswich has some of the finest examples of domestic architecture in Australia and Toowoomba, a short trip up a steep escarpment, is a truly handsome city which combines history with some excellent parks and delightful gardens.

To the east is Moreton Bay with the historic settlement of Redcliffe and the delightful islands (all of which are an easy daytrip) of Moreton Bay and to the north, a peaceful retreat from the city, is Bribie Island.

The activities available to people wanting to explore beyond the city limits are endless and include fishing, swimming, walking and exploring.

PARKS AND GARDENS
In the hills to the northwest of the city, there is a run of very attractive parks. These offer excellent views over Brisbane as well as providing tranquil walks for those wanting to escape the pressures of the city.

DON'T MISS

*** Picnic Point Lookout: on the eastern side of Toowoomba affords excellent views towards Brisbane.
*** North Stradbroke Island: noted for long, clean white beaches and the rich diversity of its flora.
*** Ipswich: some of the state's most interesting, and elegant 19th-century housing.
** Burley Griffin incinerator: the architect of Canberra built the incinerator, now a theatre at Ipswich.

Opposite: *The Tropical Dome at Mt Coot-tha Botanic Gardens houses a rich diversity of Queensland's flora.*

Mount Coot-tha Botanical Gardens and Reserve ★★★

Undoubtedly the most famous is **Mount Coot-tha Botanical Gardens and Reserve** which is located off Mount Coot-tha Road in Toowong. The Mount Coot-tha Gardens are Australia's largest subtropical display of flora. They cover 57ha (140 acres) in which plants are set against an environment of lakes, ponds, and streams. There are thousands of tropical plants housed in the unusual dome-shaped indoor displays, and growing in this veritable tropical rainforest. Of particular interest are the Japanese Gardens, an unusual cactus garden and an excellent area featuring Australian flora.

Above: Comprising 52ha (128 acres) of gardens, the Mt Coot-tha Botanic Gardens range from a Japanese garden to African plants and a special section on Australian natives.

Opposite: Laidley Pioneer Village has a well-preserved slab hut as well as an old gaol, general store, butcher's shop and a number of other interesting buildings.

Bellbird Grove ★

Bellbird Grove – 12km (7½ miles) along Mt Nebo Road from the city – is located in Camp Mountain State Forest Park which is part of the Brisbane Forest Park. This is primarily an area for people wanting to have a picnic and go for short walks in the surrounding area. There are remnants of old gold mines in the area but it is really the well-appointed adventure playground (ideal for children) and the large, comfortable picnic ground which is the major attraction.

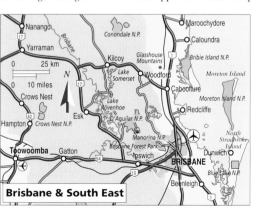

Brisbane & South East

Camp Mountain State Forest Park ★★★

Further along Mt Nebo Road is the **Camp Mountain State Forest Park** which offers some of the best views over Samford Valley. The elevation is such that it looks out over the whole of Brisbane city.

Manorina National Park ★★

Beyond the tiny township of Mt Nebo is **Manorina National Park** which allows the visitor to explore the surrounding rainforest. Visitors may also see the rich variety of wildlife which lives in this area including whipbirds and bellbirds. The best way to reach these interesting parks is to hire a car.

IPSWICH

Ipswich is a large settlement which yields its attractions only to those who are prepared to explore. It has the finest domestic architecture in Queensland. The visitor can literally drive around the streets (particularly the streets situated to the south of the business centre) and discover rows of truly magnificent and imaginatively designed old houses.

Queens Park ★★★

A good starting point is **Queens Park** which has an animal sanctuary and an attractive rotunda with delicate late Victorian cast-iron lacework. Located at the southern end of the park is the interesting **Walter Burley Griffin Incinerator** which has now been turned into a theatre.

To see some of the city's interesting architecture drive up to the top of Denmark Hill between Ellensborough Street and Murphy Street. **Lakemba is** characterised by really beautiful ironwork. It was built around the turn of the century. Around the corner, just up Ellenborough Street, is **The Foxes**, a large turn-of-the-century timber house.

Above: Toowoomba's Cobb & Co museum celebrates the horse-drawn coach service which was Queensland's major means of transportation at the end of the 19th century.

St Marys Church ★★

From Denmark Hill it is also possible to see **St Marys Catholic Church** which is one of the most substantial rural churches in the country. An awesome church, it is notable for its two Gothic spires (which can be seen from most vantage points around Ipswich), its impressive stained glasswork, its extensive use of marble, its elaborate ceilings and Italianate arches. Leave Ipswich heading west towards **Rosewood**, **Grandchester**, which has a very fine working steam sawmill, and **Laidley**, which has an interesting Historical Village that offers visitors the opportunity to inspect a range of buildings dating back to the early 19th century.

TOOWOOMBA

No Australian city is more dramatically located than Toowoomba. If you enter from the east it is clear that the city dangles on the edge of a plateau some 600–800m (2000–2700ft) above sea level. The Warrego Highway from Brisbane rises steeply up the escarpment and the city spreads from the escarpment edge to the west and south.

Toowoomba's proximity to Brisbane ensured that through the 19th century it was a popular retreat for Brisbane's powerful and wealthy residents.

Picnic Point Lookout ★★★

This should be the first stop for anyone coming from Brisbane. The Lookout offers superb views over the Lockyer Valley.

Toowoomba's **Botanic Gardens** are central to the city's annual Carnival of Flowers festivities, held for the full last week in September.

TOP ATTRACTIONS OF TOOWOOMBA

★★★ Picnic Point Lookout: on the eastern side of Toowoomba affords excellent views towards Brisbane.
★★ Drayton: is only a few kilometres from Toowoomba. Features include the Royal Bulls Head Inn built in 1847.
★★ Botanic Gardens: have outstanding floral displays throughout the year.
★★ Carnival of Flowers: held every September.

Cobb & Co Museum **

Toowoomba's most notable tourist attraction is at 27 Lindsay Street (tel: (076) 339-1971). Open from 10:00–16:00 Monday–Friday and 13:00–16:00 on weekends and public holidays. It traces the history of horse-drawn transportation in Australia from timber wagons, spring wagons, and bullock drays through to the Cobb & Co coaches.

Drayton **

The tiny settlement south west of the city can lay claim as the first town established beyond the Great Dividing Range in Queensland. It was settled in 1842 and by 1847 the **Royal Bulls Head Inn** had been built. It was a popular haunt for the local squatters and their workers.

MORETON BAY

To the east of Brisbane lies Moreton Bay with a number of islands, including Moreton and North Stradbroke. To the north is the popular fishing spot of Bribie Island.

Moreton Island ***

At various times in the last century Moreton Island was inhabited by Europeans. It was a whaling station and later became a tourist resort which was finally closed in the

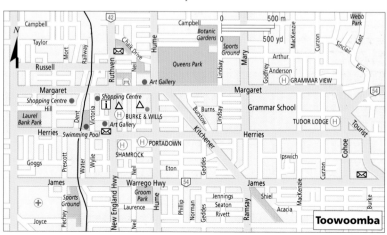

1960s. Today it is of considerable environmental interest. The 192,600ha (475,900 acres) wilderness is a rare example of a virtually untouched sand island. It has a wide range of sand island features including perched lakes, wetlands and the unusual Mount Tempest which is reputed to be the highest permanent sand dune in the world. It is also claimed that the sand dunes are the steepest in the world.

There are no established roads but 4WD vehicles can be driven on tracks along the 40km (25 mile) beach.

The most popular attraction on the island is **North Point**. The road from **Bulwer** passes through the forests of the **Moreton Island National Park** and at various points visitors may stop to admire the freshwater lakes and dunes.

The road runs to **Cape Moreton** and **North Point.** The main interest in this area is the lighthouse which was built at Cape Moreton in 1857. The first built in Queensland, it was a vital aid to shipping trying to enter the shallow and complex waters of Moreton Bay.

It is possible to drive south along the beach from the lighthouse and to join the other major road from **Bulwer** south of the **Blue Lagoon.**

North Stradbroke Island **

Located 30km (20 miles) south east of Brisbane, North Stradbroke Island and the historic settlements at **Dunwich** and **Amity Point** have become popular holiday destinations and daytripper locations for Brisbane people wanting to escape from the city.

North Stradbroke Island is noted for the long, clean white beaches of its eastern coastline, the rich diversity of its flora which includes beautiful wild orchids, and its isolation and peacefulness. Today the greatest attraction of the island is undoubtedly its impressive natural heritage.

Below: *Built in 1963, the bridge which connects Bribie Island to the mainland has increased the island's tourism. Bribie is now a popular destination for holidaymakers and fishermen.*

Blue Lake National Park ★★★

The beautiful 445ha (10,992 acres) **Blue Lake National Park**, 10km (6 miles) east of Dunwich, has an unusual freshwater table lake set in sand dunes. The lake covers 7.3ha (182 acres) and is 9.4m (31ft) at its deepest and is incredibly blue. The fauna in the park includes swamp wallabies, skinks, ospreys and the mottled tree frog, and the flora ranges from dry sclerophyll forest through heath, swamps, marshes, and scrub.

Point Lookout on Stradbroke is Queensland's most easterly point. Its steep cliffs afford an excellent **whale watching** vantage point between June and September when the humpback whales make their way past the island on their way to the breeding grounds further north.

Bribie Island ★★

Bribie Island is an interesting combination of retirement location, daytrippers fun place, family holiday retreat and haven for fishermen, sporting people (there's an excellent golf course on the island) and sun lovers.

Bribie Island and the peaceful beaches of **Beachmere**, **Woorim** and **Banksia** make an almost perfect daytrip from the city and it is largely unspoilt.

Beachmere is a place which has been largely ignored by the tourist industry which has grown up along the coast near Brisbane. There is a good beach and the fishing in the area is considered outstanding.

Woorim is a lovely ocean beach site which attracts surfers and sun lovers. It has remained relatively underdeveloped. It has a licensed hotel/motel and a caravan park and there are walks along the beaches to the north and south of the tiny township.

For those eager to escape even further from 'civilisation', the dirt roads up the Pumicestone Channel side of the island lead to the small channel beaches of **Banksia Beach** and **White Patch.** The channel is noted for its mangroves which grow at the water's edge. This means that the whole area is ideal for fishing and that an accomplished angler can expect to catch flathead, whiting and tailor.

FISHING ON BRIBIE ISLAND

Bribie Island is known for its excellent fishing. Some of the island's best locations include:
• **Pumicestone Channel:** with the small channel beaches of Banksia Beach and White Patch, which are ideal for fishing and an accomplished angler can expect to catch flathead, whiting and tailor.
• **Woorim:** an attractive ocean beach site; it is possible to catch whiting off Woorim Beach.
• **Beachmere:** known for its excellent beach, and the fishing in the area is considered outstanding.

Around Brisbane at a Glance

BEST TIMES TO VISIT

See **Brisbane at a Glance** on p. 40.

GETTING THERE

Toowoomba
Toowoomba is 128km (80 miles) from Brisbane and is well serviced by air: **Sunstate Airlines**, tel: (07) 3308-9022, toll free:13 1313. Two major coach companies, **Greyhound/Pioneer**, tel: (07) 3258-1700 or toll free 13 2030 and **McCafferty's**, tel: (07) 4960-9888 (toll free 13 1499) offer regular services from Brisbane.
Brisbane Transit Centre, tel: (07) 3236-2528, offers a speedy two-hour rail trip from Brisbane.
The road from Brisbane to Toowoomba is excellent and car hire in Brisbane is easy and relatively inexpensive.

Ipswich
Ipswich is 40km (25 miles) south west of Brisbane. It has effectively become an outer suburb of Brisbane but retains the status of a city. Highway 15 makes the journey by car fast and effortless. The electric train runs every half hour from Brisbane during the day.

Bribie Island
Is reached by driving 44km (28 miles) north from Brisbane on the Bruce Highway, turn east off the Highway and travel 19km (12 miles) further east. The island is connected to the mainland by a modern prestressed concrete bridge across Pumicestone Passage; bus service from Caboolture.

Stradbroke Island
Ferries and water taxis leave regularly from Redland Bay Marina for both North and South Stradbroke islands.
Bay Island Taxi Service, tel: (07) 3409-1145. **Stradbroke Ferries**, departs Toondah Harbour Middle Street, Cleveland, tel: (07) 3286-2666 or (018) 885226.

GETTING AROUND

Toowoomba
Toowoomba Tourist Information Centre, 86 James Street, tel: (07) 4639-3797, fax: 4639-3942, or toll free: 1800 331 155. Plan a walking or driving trip of the city.

Ipswich
Ipswich Regional Tourist Centre, cnr D'Arcy Doyle Place and Brisbane Street, tel: (07) 3281-0555, fax: 3281-0199. Offers a pamphlet called the 'Ipswich City Heritage Trails', open every day.

WHERE TO STAY

Toowoomba
Burke and Wills Hotel, 554 Ruthven Street, tel: (07) 4632-2433, (toll free) 1800 633 679, fax: (076) 4639-2002. Central.
Toowoomba Motel, 2 Burnage Street, tel: (07) 4631-8600, fax: 4631-8660. Quiet setting, all amenities.

Bridge Street Motor Inn, 291 Bridge Street, tel: (07) 4634-3299, fax: 4634-3060. Well-priced – large suites with kitchens and modern facilities.
Colonial Motel, 730 Ruthven Street, tel: (07) 4635-3233, fax: 4635-1862, (toll free) 1800 801 248. Moderately priced, short distance to city centre.

Ipswich
Sundowner Chain Motel Inn, 250 South Station Rd, tel: (07) 3202-4622, fax: 3812-1447.Well-appointed, modern motel, reasonably priced.
Ipswich Heritage Motor Inn, 51 Warwick Rd, tel: (07) 3202-3111, fax: 3202-3692. Family-style motel with pool, some rooms with kitchens.
Ipswich Flag Inn, 86 Warwick Rd, tel: (07) 3281-2633, fax: 3281-2633, (toll free) 1800 806 344. BBQ, ideal family motel, some rooms have kitchens.
Mary Ellen Motel, cnr Limestone and Thorn Streets, tel: (07) 3202-4418, fax: 3281-0772. 5 mins from city centre.

Bribie Island
Bribie Island Waterways Resort,155 Welsby Pde, Bongaree, tel: (07) 3408-3000, fax: 3408-3076, (toll free) 1800 072 080. Modern amenities, 13 units have kitchen facilities.
Koolamara Resort, Boyd Street, Woorim, tel: (07) 3408-1277, fax: 3408-1204. Close to beach and golf course this resort offers a variety of activities for the whole family.

Around Brisbane at a Glance

Holiday flats can be booked through L.J. Hooker, 30 Benabrow Ave, tel: (07) 3408-7755, fax: 3408-7820.

Stradbroke Island
Anchorage Village Beach Resort, East Coast Rd, Point Lookout, tel: (07) 3409-8266, fax: 3409-8304. Luxury units with all amenities.
Pandanus Palms Holiday Resort, Cumming Pde, Point Lookout, tel: (07) 3409-8106, fax: 3409-8339. Equipped 2- and 3-bedroom townhouses; tennis court, pool and gym.

WHERE TO EAT

Toowoomba
Ascot House, 15 Newmarket Street, tel: (07) 4633-2134. Historic mansion, one of Toowoomba's most popular restaurants, open Wed to Sun.
Weis Restaurant, 2 Margaret Street, tel: (07) 4632-7666. Elegant restaurant offering a fine selection wine.
Hogs Breath Café, 36 Neil Street, tel: (07) 4639-1400. Relaxed eating for the family.
Casa Mia Restaurant, 205 Margaret St, tel: (07) 4638-5909. Quality Italian cuisine.
Dave's Steakhouse, 732 Ruthven Street, tel: (07) 4635-0555. Steak served in a relaxed atmosphere.
Herries House Restaurant, 210 Herries Street, tel: (07) 4632-7382. Tranquil gardens surround this lovely old home creating a relaxing environment.

Ipswich
The Old Flour Mill Eatery, 231 Brisbane Street, tel: (07) 3282-8788. Fun environment plus good food in a converted flour mill, live entertainment Friday and Saturday nights.
Fentons Café Restaurant, 17 Limestone Street, tel: (07) 3812-0424. Fine food.
The Bellevue, 3 Brunett Street, tel: (07) 3812-3666. Stately colonial home offers panoramic views over Ipswich, fine cuisine is a bonus.
Go Sing, 237 Brisbane Street, tel: (07) 3281-2748. Reasonably priced Chinese cuisine boasting 'no MSG used in any meal'.

Bribie Island
Bribie Island is small and has many casual eating houses; cafés and bistros abound.

Stradbroke Island
The Stradbroke Hotel, Point Lookout, tel: (07) 3409-8188, fax: (07) 3409-8474. Two excellent restaurants offer a variety of food for the family.

TOURS AND EXCURSIONS

The Toowoomba Tourist Information Centre will help with tours and any special interests, tel: (07) 4639 3797.

Ipswich
Yellow Cabs, offers tours of the Ipswich area, tel: 13 1924.
The Tourist Information Centre will tailor individual walking tours. Buses are available for trips further afield.

Bribie Island
Bribie Island Tourist Information Centre, tel: (07) 3408-9026 will be able to help with any tour information.

Stradbroke Island
Point Lookout Scuba Dive Charter, tel: 1409 489 957.
Stradbrooke 4WD Tours, 48 Wallers Court, Point Lookout, tel: (07) 3409-8051.
An exceptional way to see the beauties of Stradbroke Island. Half day tours. Relaxed, fun and great value for money.

USEFUL CONTACTS

Toowoomba
Toowoomba Tourist Information Centre, 86 James St, tel: (07) 4639-3797, toll free: 1800 311 155.
Queensland National Parks and Wildlife Service, 158 Hume Street, Toowoomba, tel: (07) 4639-4599, fax: 4639-4524.

Ipswich
Regional Tourist Information Centre, cnr D'Arcy Doyle Pl and Brisbane Street, tel: (07) 3281-0555. Open 7 days, a range of information.

Bribie Island
The Bribie Island Tourism Information Centre, tel: (074) 3408-9026.

Stradbroke Island
Stradbroke Island Tourism, Junner Street, Dunwich, tel: (07) 3409-9555.

4
The Gold Coast

To the south east of Brisbane lies the Gold Coast which combines beautiful surf beaches, major tourist attractions and a hinterland of rainforests with tiny settlements dotted with tea houses, art and craft shops.

The Gold Coast is Australia's most famous, and probably its most successful, tourist area. From humble beginnings in the 1950s it has grown into a stretch of coastline which is almost non-stop motels and hotels, eateries, a casino and a number of high-profile attractions including **Warner Bros Movie World** and **Sea World.** It is a holiday centre where visitors from all over the world come to enjoy the sun, the lazy lifestyle and 42km (26 miles) of well-known beaches – Coolangatta, Currumbin, Palm Beach, Burleigh Heads, Nobby Beach, Mermaid Beach, Broadbeach, Surfers Paradise and Southport.

The development which has occurred along the coast has not met with universal approval. To many people the high-rise units along the beaches, the marinas, the artificial waterways, and the multi-million dollar developments all smack of environmental insensitivity.

In spite of these reservations, the area continues to act as a magnet. Its population doubles every decade. It attracts hundreds of thousands of holidaymakers during the summer and its New Year's Eve celebrations have become legendary for their public displays of high spirits. Its appeal lies in the way it has concentrated a large number of holiday activities – swimming and surfing, a mild to warm climate, a variety of accommodation and plenty of family activities, in a relatively small area.

DON'T MISS

*** **Currumbin Sanctuary:** noted for the rainbow lorikeets which flock there at feeding time.
** **Movie World:** a movie theme park similar to Universal Studios in Hollywood.
** **Conrad International Hotel and Jupiters Casino:** a wide variety of gambling.
** **Surfers Paradise:** the most famous beach on the Gold Coast.

Opposite: *This is the Gold Coast, Queensland's most popular tourist destination, a strip of golden sand and a seemingly endless run of hotels and apartment blocks.*

Opposite above:

*On the headland between
Tweed Heads and Coolan-
gatta stands a memorial
to Captain Cook and a
lighthouse which has been
turned into a celebration
of Cook's exploration
of the coast.*

COOLANGATTA

Coolangatta is the most southerly of all of the holiday
destinations on the Gold Coast. It is realistically a twin
town with Tweed Heads. The border between New
South Wales and Queensland is now so blurred at this
point that people pass from one state to the next barely
noticing that they are crossing a border.

The area was explored by John Oxley who discovered and named the Tweed River in 1823. The town
was actually named after the ship called *Coolangatta*,
which was wrecked on the coast in the 1840s. It is said
that the word was an Anglicised Aboriginal word
meaning 'beautiful place'.

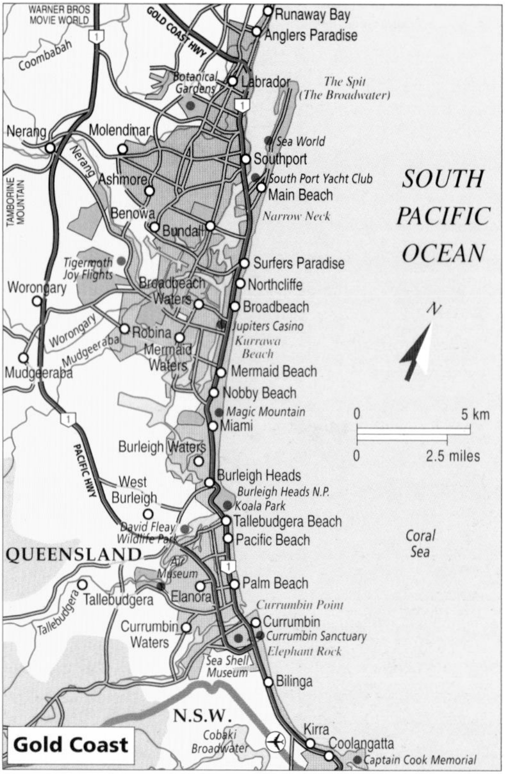

The Gold Coast's oldest
holiday destination, the
town is more relaxed
and family orientated than
other coastal parts. Attractions range from the beach
to sightseeing, going to see
a movie and travelling to
the Currumbin Sanctuary,
up the coast.

Point Danger *

An excellent vantage point
is Point Danger. Captain
James Cook named **Point
Danger** and a lighthouse
was built to warn ships.
The lighthouse is now a
memorial to Cook. It lays
claim to being the first
lighthouse in the world to
experiment with laser technology but the experiment
was unsuccessful and it
returned to the conven-
tional mirrors, magnifying
glass and electric lamps.

Gold Coast

GOLD COAST – TIME LINE

Before 1788 Aborigines recognised the area for its excellent fishing grounds.
1888 A hotel was built but the only access from the north was by ferry across the Nerang River at Southport.
1923 James Cavill paid £40 for a block of land and proceeded to build his famous Surfers Paradise Hotel.
1925 A wooden bridge was built across the Nerang River giving access to the hotel which boasted a small zoo and excellent gardens.
1940s Surfers Paradise Hotel was used during World War II by convalescing soldiers.
1950s Soldiers returned with their wives and families to enjoy the beach and the excellent climate.

Currumbin Sanctuary ★★★

To the north is **Currumbin**, famous for the excellent **Currumbin Sanctuary** in Tomewin Street. Rainbow lorikeets flock there at feeding time. Over the years this simple bird sanctuary has grown so that now it includes a wildlife reserve which houses kangaroos, wallabies, koalas and emus. There is also a range of tourist attractions including glass blowing and a miniature railway. In many ways it is one of the most impressive attractions on the Gold Coast.

Burleigh Heads National Park ★★

North of Currumbin, the 24ha (59 acres) park is actually an isolated extension of a huge volcano which was centred at Mount Warning 22 million years ago. Given the development that has gone on around it, the park has managed to preserve a small area of coastal rainforest and heath lands. There is a short, well-maintained, 3km (2 mile) track which offers superb views of the coast. The park is the habitat for wallabies, koalas and bandicoots but you will be lucky to see them.

Below: *Millions of tourists visit Surfers Paradise each year to enjoy its casino, beaches and beach cafés and restaurants.*

Above: *The premier hotel on the Gold Coast is the Marina Mirage located at The Spit or The Broadwater near the marina and Sea World.*

David Fleay Wildlife Park ★★

A few kilometres west of the coast on West Burleigh Road is **David Fleay Wildlife Park.** This is an opportunity to observe the native fauna of the area in a zoo environment. The fauna centre is home to crocodiles, cassowaries, and brolgas. There is a special area for children. For more information contact Fleay's (tel: (07) 5576 2411).

SURFERS PARADISE

Both a town and a beach, **Surfers Paradise** symbolises the lifestyle and the aspirations of the people who come to the Gold Coast either to holiday or to live. The origins of the modern town really date to 1923 when James Cavill paid £40 for a block of land and built his famous Surfers Paradise Hotel.

The great change in the area occurred in the 1950s. The Surfers Paradise Hotel had been used during World War II by convalescing soldiers who now returned with their wives and families to enjoy the beach and the excellent climate. Today it has the greatest concentration of five-star hotels in Queensland outside Brisbane.

SOUTHPORT

Southport is the newest and most expensive area of the Gold Coast. Out on the narrow area known as The Spit or The Broadwater there is a superb new marina, **Sea World** and the **Sheraton Mirage Hotel.**

CLIMATE

The Gold Coast is far enough south to be an ideal holiday destination during the spring, summer and autumn months. It is too far south to be affected by box jellyfish and rarely experiences the tropical cyclonic weather which affects the Far North in summer. In winter the weather can be quite cool and people holidaying during the winter months will most often opt for heated hotel and motel pools rather than surfing. The winter days are often sunny and mild.

Southport grew in the 1870s and 1880s. The Southport Hotel was built in 1876. A pier was constructed in 1880 and the area known as Main Beach (where the Sheraton Mirage is located) was sold in 1885.

The development of the area since World War I has been continuous. The bridge over the Nerang River was completed in 1925 giving easy access to the area. Prior to that the only access to The Broadwater had been by ferry.

Southport Area

Map locations: Labrador, Wave Break Island, Nerang Head, Heydon Heights, Botanical Gardens, The Spit (The Broadwater), Albert Shire Council Chambers, Sea World, Marina Mirage Resort, Bungee Downunder, Molendinar, Southport, Fishermans Wharf, Nerang, Ashmore, South Port Yacht Club, Main Beach, Paradise Waters, Narrow Neck, Chevron Island, Benowa, Worongary, Tigermoth Joy Flights, Gold Coast Turf Club, Surfers Paradise, Carrara, Bundall, Northcliffe, Benowa Waters, Cascades Parks & Gardens, Merrimac, Broadbeach Waters, Jupiters Casino, Broadbeach, Kurrawa Beach, Pacific Fair

97, 90

0   2 km
0   1 mile

N

Today the Southport area concentrates entirely on tourism. The hotels and apartments in the area are substantially more expensive and more luxurious than the facilities further south. The main activities available to visitors still depend on the beach. Southport beach is ideal for surfing and, because it is firm and flat, it is perfect for a pleasant walk.

The Spit or The Broadwater offers a variety of activities – most of which spill over from Sea World. There is bungee jumping, a number of quality fast-food outlets

Left: *The Gold Coast has a number of family-orientated theme parks including Sea World, Dreamworld, Movie World, Koala Town and Wet'n'Wild Cades County.*

Above: *North of the Gold Coast is Sanctuary Cove, a five-star resort located on a series of artificial canals which ensure that every dwelling enjoys water views.*
Opposite: *A quiet retreat from the Gold Coast is Tamborine Mountain. It is famed for its tea houses, forests, panoramic views, and waterfalls like the Curtis Falls.*

JUPITERS CASINO

Jupiters was Queensland's first casino. Located at Broadbeach on the Gold Coast, it is part of the A$206 million Conrad International Hotel development, and offers gamblers a wide range of activities from the conventional Baccarat, Roulette and Blackjack tables to Australian Two-up and the popular Japanese games Keno and Sic-Bo. The casino is an easy walk from the beach.

(particularly good are the seafood cafés) and parasailing. The **Sheraton Mirage** is recognised as the best hotel on the Gold Coast not only because of its five-star rating but because of its easy access to the beach and its excellent swimming and sunbathing facilities.

Sea World ★★★

Sea World on The Spit, Main Beach, is one of the premier commercial attractions on the Gold Coast. Its large parking area, and its convenient location opposite the Sheraton Mirage, ensure its popularity. This huge 25ha (62 acres) marine park (the largest of its kind in Australia) is a combination of performing dolphins and whales, aqua-ballet and rides on such hair-raising machines as the Three Loop Corkscrew and Lasseters Lost Mine. Like most of the major, multi-million dollar attractions on the Gold Coast, it is designed to entertain the entire family for an entire day.

Warner Bros Movie World ★★★

With some justification, Movie World has been promoted as the premier family attraction on the Gold Coast. This huge complex is a combination of working studios (the main activities are advertisements and small budget movies) and a theme park which seems to have been modelled on the Universal City Studio Tours in Hollywood. The usual wide collection of eateries are available on Main Street. Actors wander around in various disguises ranging from police to thieves and there are a number of set-piece shows including a kind of 'Police Academy' stunt show, a Wild West show and various adventure rides through well-known movie sets. Of most interest is the area where the blue screen (the device used for back projection which gives the illusion of danger) and other cinematic tricks are explained. It takes a full day to see and experience everything. The entry fee covers all the activities inside.

Conrad International Hotel and Jupiters Casino ★★

Broadbeach, which lies just a few kilometres south of Surfers Paradise, boasts the A$185 million **Conrad International Hotel** and **Jupiters Casino** complex with its gaming rooms, swimming pools, tennis courts and jogging tracks. Opened in 1986 it has over 600 guest rooms and is the only casino on the Gold Coast. Rare among casinos, it operates 24 hours a day allowing the gambler to lose money as easily at 5am as at 5pm.

Jupiters Casino is where popular Japanese gambling games like Keno and Sic-Bo (designed to appeal to the increasing number of Japanese tourists) vie with Baccarat, Roulette, Blackjack and the all-Australian Two-up.

Other high-class hotels include **Sanctuary Cove** and the low-rise luxury of the **Sheraton Mirage Gold Coast** with its marina and lagoon. The **Twin Towns RSL Club** has built a A$16 million sports complex with an 18-hole golf course, tennis courts and an Olympic-sized swimming pool. The **Wet'n'Wild Water World** features the only man-made pool in Australia with one-metre waves and lifeguards. The A$400 million **Sanctuary Cove** boasts an 18-hole golf course designed by the champion golfer Arnold Palmer.

HINTERLAND ATTRACTIONS

Behind the Gold Coast the escarpment rises sharply to a cool mountain region characterised by tea rooms and gift shops. Pay a visit to **Tamborine Mountain** with its rainforest (the **Joalah National Park**) and its road along the ridge which is bordered by craft shops, devonshire tea houses, galleries, and florists. Further along the ridge is **Wilsons Lookout** which has outstanding views to the east over the city of the Gold Coast and **Rotary Lookout** which is located on the western side of the mountain range. Nearby are the **Cedar Creek Falls** in the **Cedar Creek National Park**.

ROUND TRIP TO NEW SOUTH WALES

A rewarding circular day trip from the Gold Coast can be taken into New South Wales. Leave **Southport**, travel through **Nerang** and up to Natural Bridge. From there the road crosses into New South Wales. The views south from the border fence are particularly impressive. The road drops down to the tiny village of **Chillingham** and then follows the Tweed River through fields of sugar cane to the town of **Murwillumbah**. The journey from Murwillumbah to the Gold Coast passes through the Tweed's alluvial valley before reaching **Tweed Heads** and **Coolangatta** where high-rise development of the Gold Coast begins.

THE HINTERLAND

Looking at the golden beaches and the seemingly endless high-rise apartment blocks and hotels, it's hard to imagine that in the hinterland behind the Gold Coast there are stretches of unspoilt rainforest, spectacular waterfalls and the beautifully rugged **Lamington National Park**. The visitor who decides to travel up to the mountains will be amazed by the contrast. The peacefulness of the villages and the quaintness of· the tea and craft shops stand in sharp contrast to the exuberance of the coast.

Tamborine Mountain ★★

Tamborine Mountain is really a collective term for a number of small villages (**Eagle Heights**, **North Tamborine**, **Mountain Tamborine**) and settlements stretching along the ridge of the mountain range. One of the appeals of the hinterland is the quiet gift shops and attractive tea houses sprinkled along the main roads on Tamborine Mountain. There are also outstanding views to the east of the city of the Gold Coast from **Wilsons Lookout**. The high-rise buildings on the horizon form a strangely serrated skyline.

Canungra ★

Canungra is a small, thriving township at the southern end of the **Tamborine Mountain National Park**. The town describes itself as the 'Gateway to the Mountains'. Visitors intending to explore the area should stop at the **North Tamborine Information Centre**, tel: (07) 5545-1171 – for maps and information on walks and sightseeing.

Canungra is a quiet township located on Canungra Creek. Like much of the Tamborine Mountain area it survives by selling gifts and providing meals for the visitors who make their way up the mountain.

The attractions of the area are the beautiful views which exist on both sides of the ranges and the number of rainforest areas with quiet streams and attractive waterfalls. From the ridge it is possible to get excellent views to both the west and the east.

Witches Falls National Park ★★

The **Witches Falls National Park** lays claim to being the first national park to be declared in the state. It was established in 1908. The **Rotary Lookout** offers dramatic views west towards Beaudesert and Boonah.

Rainforest and Waterfalls

The Tamborine Mountain area is ideal for people who want to bushwalk and explore the countryside. Its beauty is in its views and its rainforests. About 5km (3 miles) from North Tamborine is **Thunderbird Park** a well-presented and well-organised tourist retreat which provides visitors with everything from a mine, where visitors can go fossicking, to mini golf, a pub, souvenir shops and excellent motel-style accommodation, and further down the hill is **Cedar Creek National Park** which offers one of the most delightful walks in the whole Tamborine area. The easy walk is only a few hundred metres to the **Cedar Creek Falls** in the Cedar Creek National Park which tumble (gently rather than spectacularly) down into a gully. There are a number of good walks through the rainforest.

Other attractions in the area include **Natural Bridge** and the beautiful **Lamington National Park** both of which are well worth visiting.

Above: *The view across Numinbah Valley from Nyoogai Lookout in the Lamington National Park is a far cry from the high-rise of the Gold Coast which is less than 50km (31 miles) to the east.*

NATURAL BRIDGE

One of the Gold Coast's premier natural attractions is the **Natural Bridge** phenomenon at **Cave Creek**. Visitors walk through rainforests to a narrow creek and, at one end of the walk, the river disappears into a huge hole in the roof of a cave to emerge below in a water pool. The national park around Natural Bridge is noted for its shady groves, rich bird life and rainforest stands of hoop pines.

The Gold Coast at a Glance

The Gold Coast enjoys year round temperate weather. December to early February is considered the 'wet' season. June through August is officially winter, and the nights can get chilly especially in the hinterland.

The Gold Coast is a 42km (26 miles) strip running from Coolangatta in the south to Southport in the north. Coolangatta has its own airport and the major airlines, **Ansett**, tel: 131 300 and **Qantas**, tel: 131 313, fly in regularly. There are several shuttle bus services from the airport which, in most cases, will drop the visitor off at most hotels. Check at the airport information booth. Car rental companies operate from the airport. **Regent Taxis** serve the Gold Coast, tel: 13 1008.

The Gold Coast, Surfers Paradise, Coolangatta and Southport are easily accessible by public transport. **Southport Transit Centre**, Scarborough St, Southport, tel: (07) 5591-2587, runs a 24hr service up and down the coast. **Gold Coast Tourist Shuttle**, tel, toll free: 1300 655 655, offer all-day tickets which will take you to the coast's major attractions.

Car rental is fairly cheap and easy on the coast with a vast number of companies operating in the area: **Red Back Rentals**, tel: (07) 5592-1655, **Delta**, tel: 13 1390, **Rent-a-Jeep**, tel: (07) 5538-6900.

Coolangatta
Serviced Apartments are very popular on the Gold Coast and cost no more than motel-type accommodation. **Beachcomber International Resort**, 122 Griffith Street, tel: (07) 5574-2800, fax: 5574-2810. Two swimming pools, gym and luxury serviced apartments makes this an ideal base in Coolangatta. **Carool Luxury Apartments**, 5 Eden Ave, tel: (07) 5536-7154, fax: 5536 7204. Apartments with magnificent views and every luxury. **Beach House Seaside Resort**, 52-58 Marine Parade, tel: (07) 5574 2800, fax: 5574-2810. Luxury family apartments with spectacular views of Coolangatta Beach, centrally located to both the shops and the airport.

BUDGET
Bombora on the Park, 4 Carmichael Cl, tel: (07) 5536-1888, fax: 5536-1828. This parkland setting offers not only nightly accommodation but packages which include 3-course dinner and breakfast; a family favourite at an affordable price.

Surfers Paradise
ANA Hotel Gold Coast, 22 View Ave, tel: (07) 5579-1000, fax: 5570-1260. Luxury hotel with every facility in the heart of Surfers Paradise.

Marriott Resort, 158 Ferny Avenue, tel: (07) 5592-9800, fax: 5592-9888, toll free 008 809 090. Large family rooms, luxury facilities and free shuttle bus to the major attractions.
Capricorn One Apartments, 198 Ferny Ave, tel: (07) 5570-2344, fax: 5531-5373. Self-contained units with resort facilities and water views.
Beachpoint Oceanfront Apartments, cnr Staghorn Ave and The Esplanade, tel: (07) 5538-4355, fax: 55709299. Ocean views, luxury 2-bedroom apartments with both indoor and outdoor pools.

BUDGET
Trickett Gardens Holiday Inn, 24-30 Trickett Street, tel: (07) 5539-0988, fax: 5592-0791, toll free 008 07 4290. Low-rise serviced apartment building in the heart of Surfers Paradise well appointed, reasonably priced.

Southport
Sheraton Mirage, Seaworld Drive, Main Beach, tel: (07) 5591-1488, fax: 5591-2299. The ultimate luxury resort offering fabulous high class accommodation and high-class dining.

The Gold Coast at a Glance

Park Regis, 2 Barney St, tel: (07) 5532-7922, fax: 5532-0195. Located on the Broadwater this well-appointed hotel offers modern facilities.

BUDGET

Earls Court Motor Inn, 131 Nerang Street, tel: (07) 5591-4144, fax: 5591-1658. This small motel is conveniently located with pool and BBQ area.

Swan Lane Apartments, cnr Queen Street and Swan Lane, tel: (07) 5532-1811, fax: 5531-3638. Well appointed apartments, reasonably priced, close to shopping.

WHERE TO EAT

The Gold Coast has a wide selection of restaurants. They offer the traveller a variety which ranges from elegant cuisine to fast foods.

Coolangatta

The Aztec, 1st floor Showcase Building Marine Parade, tel: (07) 5599-2748. Authentic Mexican cuisine in a relaxed and colourful atmosphere.

Beaches Restaurant, cnr Warner and Marine Pdes, tel: (07) 5536-9311. This award-winning seafood restaurant offers inside and outside dining right on the beach.

Earth 'n' Sea, Marine Parade, tel: (07) 5536-3477. Italian restaurant that prides itself on fresh ingredients and friendly service.

Thai Star, 3 Griffith Street, tel: (07) 5536-6202. Authentic Thai cooking.

Surfers Paradise

Shogun Japanese Karaoke Restaurant, 90 Blundell Road, tel: (07) 5538-2872. Teppanyaki at its very best. The atmosphere is fun and the food is simply delicious.

La Rustica Italian Restaurant, 3118 Gold Coast Highway, tel: (07) 5570-1153. Quality Italian restaurant, with a friendly atmosphere.

Margarita's Restaurant, 150 Bundall Rd, tel: (07) 5592-2100. Award-winning restaurant – a wide selection of fresh food served with the authentic touch of Mexico.

Southport

Grumpy's Wharf, 60–70 Seaworld Drive, Main Beach, tel: (07) 5532-2900. A steak and seafood restaurant overlooking the beautiful marina.

Mirage Gold Coast Resort, Seaworld Dr, Main Beach, tel: (07) 5591-1488, refer to **Where to Stay** *(see* p. 62). Several restaurants are a part of this resort all offering excellent cuisine from the elegant to the casual.

TOURS AND EXCURSIONS

The Gold Coast offers a wide variety of tours and excursions from adventure to conducted tours.

The **Gold Coast Tourism Bureau** offer extensive information to suit everyone, tel: (07) 5592-2699.

Tall Ship Sailing Cruise, Sea World Drive, Main Beach, bookings, tel: (07) 5532-2444. Offers a variety of cruises, with a pick up and delivery coach service.

Trailseeker Tours, tel: 5528-3271, or 0418 453 790. Small groups with guided walking tours and morning tea.

Southern Cross 4WD Tours, tel, toll free: 1800 067 367. Tours with a difference, taking the traveller through some of the most beautiful hinterland in Queensland.

Lamington National Park Visitor Information Centre, tel: (07) 5533-3548, fax: 5533-3767. Complete information on park activities, walks and maps.

USEFUL CONTACTS

Gold Coast Tourism Bureau, Head Office, Level 2, 64 Ferny Ave, Surfers Paradise. tel: (07) 5592-2699.

Information Centre, Beach House, Marine Parade, Coolangatta. tel: (07) 5536-7765. Cavill Mall, Surfers Paradise, tel: (07) 5538-4419.

Queensland National Parks and Wildlife Service, 1711 Gold Coast Highway, Burleigh Heads. tel: (07) 5535-3032.

5
The Sunshine Coast

Although Queensland's Gold Coast has long been considered the state's premier tourist destination, the development of the Sunshine Coast (an area of beaches and hinterland about 100km (61 miles) north of Brisbane) has become a serious competitor since the 1980s. Mainstream attractions like **The Big Pineapple** (a theme park based around pineapple production) and the **Macadamia Nut Factory**, natural wonders like the volcanic plugs known as the **Glasshouse Mountains** and the peaceful beauty of **Noosa Heads National Park**, and a string of excellent **beaches** starting at Caloundra and culminating in the very up-market beaches at Noosa Heads have all helped to make the area one of the most desirable holiday and retirement destinations on the Queensland coast.

Development of this area has been extensive. At Noosa Heads there are homes, apartments and holiday accommodation worth millions of dollars. The development of the town has made it a centre of cafés and up-market clothes shops rather than the usual Australian beach resort staple of ice cream parlours and cafés selling meat pies, milk shakes and sandwiches.

Maroochydore and Mooloolaba are characterised by a more typical beach culture. High-rise apartments and modestly priced motels abound, the beach is the centre of all activities and the holidaymakers are attracted by the warm weather and good beach conditions.

Inland villages and towns provide gift shops and tea houses and attractions include parks, bushwalking, waterfalls and vantage points for viewing the distant coastline.

DON'T MISS

*** Glasshouse Mountains: impressive volcanic plugs rising out of pineapple fields.
*** Gympie Museum: one of the most impressive historical museums in Australia.
*** Gympie WoodWorks Forestry and Timber Museum: a fascinating museum about timber.
** Noosa National Park: a beautiful nature retreat in the middle of the Sunshine Coast.
** The Big Pineapple: one of the best of the theme parks on the Sunshine Coast.

Opposite: *Beerwah, the highest of the ten trachyte Glasshouse Mountains.*

Opposite above: *A series of volcanic plugs, the Glasshouse Mountains stand surrounded by farmlands and pineapple plantations a few kilometres inland from the Sunshine Coast.*
Opposite below: *On the Sunshine Coast it is easy to escape from the tourism. The unspoilt Moffat Beach is only a short distance north of Caloundra.*

THE GLASSHOUSE MOUNTAINS

Captain James Cook was the first European to see the remarkable Glasshouse Mountains. He named them because they 'very much resemble a glass house, and for this reason I called them the Glass Houses'. Today they have become one of the premier tourist attractions on the Sunshine Coast. They are not only important to the European history of southern Queensland, but play a major part in the Aboriginal culture of the area.

The Glasshouse Mountains are a series of volcanic plugs (the surrounding material has been slowly eroded away) of rhyolite and trachyte estimated to be between 24 and 25 million years old. There are actually 13 volcanic plugs in the area but only 10 dominate the landscape.

The only plug (mountain) which can be climbed quite easily is **Ngungun**. The wildlife of the area, which ranges from koalas and wallabies to echidnas and lizards, is bountiful.

Glasshouse Mountains Lookout ★★★

The best place to get an overall view of the area is the **Glasshouse Mountains Lookout**. All of the major volcanic plugs can be seen. They are placed in the context of the whole area – the lookout is high enough to see the sea. There are descriptive placards and signs to help the visitor to identify each mountain.

According to Aboriginal legend **Tibrogargan** (which is 282m/716ft high) the father and **Beerwah** (at

CLIMATE

The Sunshine Coast is marginally warmer than Brisbane. It is the southern-most part of the Queensland coast which enjoys good weather all year round. The average summer temperatures range from 17°C–28°C (62°F–82°F). Temperatures may rise above 30°C (86°F) but it is modified by on-shore breezes near the coast. In spring and autumn the temperature drops to 13°C–25°C (55°F–77°F) and in winter the daily average ranges from 7°C (86°F) at night to 22°C (86°F) during the day.

555m/1820ft, the highest peak) the mother, had a number of children of whom **Coonowrin** (375m/1230ft – narrow and most dramatic) was the eldest, **Tunbubudla** were the twins (293m/961ft and 312m/1023ft) and the rest were **Coochin** (238m/780ft), **Ngungun** (236m/774ft), **Tibberoowuccum** (205m/676ft), **Miketeebumulgrai** (199m/653ft) and **Elimbah** (129m/423ft).

CALOUNDRA

In recent times Caloundra has become a mixture of young commuters to Brisbane, holidaymakers and retired people.

With its 13km (8 miles) of delightful beaches – **Curramundi**, **Dicky**, **Moffatt**, **Shelly**, **Kings**, **Bulcock** and **Golden Beach** – its greenery, its near perfect climate, and its easy lifestyle, Caloundra is the most southerly resort on the Sunshine Coast.

The city has a number of tourist attractions including a ⅔-size replica of **Cook's H.M. Barque** *Endeavour* which is located at 3 Landsborough Parade (on the way to Golden Beach), and the **Caloundra Lighthouse**, built on the top of Canberra Terrace in 1898 and was moved to its present site in 1970. It is currently owned by the National Trust. The **Queensland Air Museum** is located at the Caloundra Aerodrome.

MAROOCHYDORE

Maroochydore is a classic Queensland coastal holiday destination with virtually continuous development – high-rise blocks of flats and units interspersed with lower development and housing dating from the 1950s – stretching down the coast to Caloundra. It is the very heart of the Sunshine Coast. A perfect holiday destination with kilometres of golden beaches, pleasant beach parks, small shopping centres geared to the tourists, some small industrial development in the hinterland, and a sense of holidays in the air all year round. The beach is the town's main attraction but, for those looking for something truly different, there is also the **Bli Bli Castle** which sits perched on a hill near the ocean between Noosa and Maroochydore. It is open from 09:00–17:00 and for further details, tel: (07) 5448-5373.

GYMPIE

Gympie is a complex and unwieldy town which stretches along the Bruce Highway for 5–6km (3–4 miles). Gympie proclaims proudly that it was **'The Town that saved Queensland'**. In 1867 Queensland, less than a decade old, was facing possible bankruptcy when James Nash discovered gold near the present site of Gympie. Overnight the wealth from the goldfield (it was to produce over 99 million grams/3.5 million ounces of gold) led to Queensland's first gold rush and pulled the state back from potential disaster.

Gympie has two superb tourist attractions which should not be missed.

GYMPIE'S MUSEUM

Gympie has two superb museums. The Gold and Mining Museum is set in attractive parklands which are ideal for picnics, and The WoodWorks Forestry and Timber Museum is one of the best working museums in Australia. Both are located on the Bruce Highway and clearly signposted.
The Gold and Mining Museum is an outstanding folk museum with an interesting range of buildings. It is open daily from 09:00–17:00 and detailed brochures on the buildings in the complex are provided with each entry ticket, tel: (07) 5482-3995.
The WoodWorks Forestry and Timber Museum has old tools and equipment including bullock wagons used in the early timber industry and timber sample displays of 101 species, tel: (07) 5483-7691.

The Gold and Mining Museum ***

The Gold and Mining Museum is spread over a number of hectares, distinguished from the road by its reproduction of a mine headframe and gantry. The buildings in the complex range from old school houses to a blacksmith's shop and the displays include an old camera and movie room, a trophy room celebrating Gympie's sporting achievements, and a dairy display.

The WoodWorks Forestry and Timber Museum ***

The WoodWorks Forestry and Timber Museum is truly interactive. Outside there are displays of pit sawing, cross-cut sawing (visitors can have a try), there is a timber cutters bark hut, a shelter shed with shingle roof, a blacksmith's shop and a steam-driven saw mill. There are demonstrations of the old tools by experienced timber cutters and explanations of the transport equipment. The steam-driven sawmill is only operated about eight times a year and for dates it is wise to contact the Museum tel: (07) 5483-7691. The working demonstrations of pit sawing and cross-cut sawing and other timber cutting activities are held on Wednesdays at 10:00 am and 13:00 pm and Sundays at 14:00 pm.

BEYOND THE COAST

Beyond the Sunshine Coast lie the Eumundi Ranges with its peaceful villages, green pastures and views across the hinterland to the ocean. A day trip into the mountains is an escape from the development and tourism of the coast.

Kenilworth **

This tiny settlement is noted more as a bushwalkers retreat than a township. The area has a number of streams and waterfalls and the local fauna includes skinks, sugar gliders and an interesting variety of birds.

MALENY FESTIVAL

With that special logic often attached to unusual fetes and festivals, the Maleny Festival is now held at Woodford in January. It is one of the most successful folk–cultural festivals in Australia attracting crowds of more than 20,000 and featuring both international acts and exceptional local performers. It is common for troupes of Aboriginal dancers to travel thousands of kilometres to participate in this unique event.

Opposite: *In 1867 Gympie was saved by the discovery of gold. This is celebrated in the town's statues and its excellent Gold and Mining Museum.*
Below: *With views across the Sunshine Coast, the pioneer cottage (now a museum) at Buderim is a reminder of the region's agricultural past.*

Kenilworth Historic Homestead offers adventure holidays with horse riding, bushwalking, swimming and canoeing, and fossicking for gemstones. The Kenilworth Country Foods Cheese Factory has both tours and tastings and the interesting Movie Museum.

Mapleton Falls **

Mapleton is perched on the top of the mountain range behind Nambour. Its chief attractions are the lily ponds and the **Mapleton Falls** in the Mapleton National Park. The park is quite small (26ha/64 acres) but the lookout from the falls (which tumble down the cliff face for 120m/394ft rather than fall sheer) offers excellent views over the valley which is covered with dense rainforest. The National Park has a number of interesting rainforest walks.

Flaxton **

Flaxton is probably the prettiest of all the Blackall Range settlements. It has a golf course, mountain accommodation and some rather beautiful arts and crafts shops. It offers access to **Kondalilla Falls** which are part of the small (327ha/807 acres) Kondalilla National Park with remnants of wet eucalypt and subtropical rainforest. The Kondalilla Falls tumble 80m (262ft) over the escarpment to a series of beautiful pools popular as swimming spots.

Below: *Noosa Heads is notable for its coffee lounges and exclusive boutiques which give it a level of sophistication that makes it quite unlike other seaside resorts.*

Buderim ***

Buderim has become a kind of Sunshine Coast hill station. It is a cool and luxuriant town characterised by gardens in which there are profusions of hibiscus, bougainvillea, poincianas and frangipani. In 1876 a sugar mill was built and in that same year the beautiful **Pioneer Cottage**, now the home of the Buderim Historical Society, was built by John Burnett out of pit sawn cedar and beech.

NOOSA
Noosa Heads ***

Noosa Heads is an island of sophistication in a huge area of beach tourism. The first European to come to Noosa to 'get away from it all' was the convict 'Wandi' (David Bracefell) who managed to escape from Moreton Bay with almost monotonous regularity. Each time he escaped he fled north and lived with the Noosa Aborigines. Between 1828–1839 he escaped four times.

Left: *The view from Laguna Lookout, south east of the Noosa township, reaches beyond the Noosa estuary to the grazing pastures of the hinterland.*

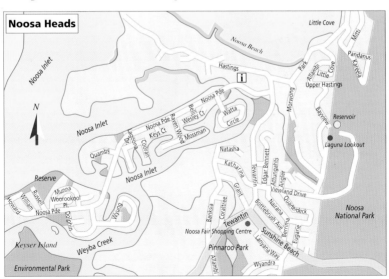

Above: *The Sunshine Coast hinterland has a number of theme parks and attractions based on the produce of the area – ginger, sugar cane, pineapples, macadamia nuts, honey. The Big Pineapple near Nambour is the largest and most successful of these attractions.*

It wasn't until after World War I that the area began to develop as a tourist resort. A surf lifesaving club was formed in 1927, the Noosa National Park was established in 1930 and tourist development started in earnest in the late 1940s.

The road which winds along the banks of the Noosa River from **Tewantin** provides a number of picnic spots beside the river. While Tewantin is the older settlement, today the two tourist destinations merge into each other and it is only the newness and cost of Noosa which really divides them.

There is a ferry at Tewantin which crosses the river and a gravel road leads to **Teewah Beach** which is famed for its coloured sands. The sandy cliffs, which can be up to 200m (656ft) in height, are made up of as many as 72 different coloured sands which have been produced by combinations of iron oxide and leached vegetable dyes. It is likely that the sands have been forming since the last ice age. It is claimed that the Aborigines had a story which explained the sands in terms of the killing of a rainbow by a huge boomerang.

Noosa National Park **

The **Noosa National Park**, located on the headland beyond Little Cove, is a small coastal park of 382ha (942 acres) in which birds and small mammals find refuge in the native flora. The bushwalks and picnic spots are a quiet retreat from the tourism of the surrounding area.

South of Noosa there are a number of attractive surf beaches including **Sunshine Beach**, **Marcus Beach**, **Peregian Beach** and **Coolum**. Each has its own charm. It is common for Australians to select a beach based on the size of the crowd at any particular time and whether the surf looks inviting.

Coolum **

Coolum is a typical beach resort town with lots of high-rise buildings. The popularity of the area is a combination of the unspoilt cliff faces of **Mount Coolum** and the beautiful beaches which are a magnet for surfers all year round.

The beach is long and clean. There is a surf patrol which operates through the summer months.

The Big Pineapple **

The big commercial attraction on the Sunshine Coast is the Big Pineapple which is a typical Queensland tourist theme park. It is a place to spend money on tropical fruits and gifts while clambering up the **Big Pineapple** (it is 16m/52ft high), taking a ride on a train through the **Tropical Plantation**, hopping aboard the **Nutmobile** for a journey through 'Nutcountry', or visiting the **Animal Nursery**. It has a licensed restaurant, a special macadamia display, and a huge greenhouse all of which are designed to entertain the visitor. The gift shops are full of pineapple drinks, dried pineapples and macadamia nuts packaged in every way imaginable.

The Ginger Factory *

The Ginger Factory is primarily a factory which produces the bulk of the world's ginger for confectionery. It is interesting and informative to stand on the observation platform at the factory and watch the processes involved in producing ginger. The owners have created a total tourist experience where, after you have bought ginger in every possible shape and size, you can go on a river cruise on the *P. S. Ginger Belle*, see a video on the Australian Ginger Industry, check out a doll's museum or board the **Ginger Bus** for a tour of a ginger farm.

> **BEST BEACHES ON THE SUNSHINE COAST**
>
> Between Caloundra and Noosa Heads there are a run of excellent beaches. Particularly popular are **Sunshine Beach**, **Peregian Beach** and **Coolum Beach** which all lie directly south of **Noosa Heads**. Each has its own access and they are not usually crowded. The beaches at **Noosa**, **Maroochydore** and **Mooloolaba** are more accessible and consequently attract large crowds in summertime. Each of these beaches has a surf life saving club. It is always sensible to swim between the flags on the patrolled section of the beach.

Below: *Tourists are protected by surf lifesavers on most of the Sunshine Coast's beaches. The clubs have regular friendly competitions to test their surfing prowess.*

The Sunshine Coast at a Glance

The Sunshine Coast has an average of seven hours of sun per day. Summer sees the temperature climb to an average of 25°C with warm nights (December to February). This is officially the 'wet' season and showers during the day can occur. March to November offers temperate weather. Through most of the winter months it is warm enough to swim and enjoy the sun.

The Bruce Highway is the main artery through the Sunshine Coast. Caloundra, which is 98km (61 miles) north of Brisbane, is on the southern tip of the region.
Major coach companies offer regular interstate service and a daily service from Brisbane. **Greyhound/Pioneer**, tel: 13 2030 and **McCafferty's** tel: 13 1499. These are toll free numbers. The main northern railway line, linking Brisbane with the State's far north, passes through the heart of the Sunshine Coast. There are regular services to Maroochydore and Noosa from Brisbane.

Car rentals in Queensland are quite inexpensive. Caloundra, Maroochydore and Noosa Heads are off the Bruce Highway. The coast road from Caloundra to Noosa is an easy drive, 56km (34 miles) in total.

Caloundra
Norm Provans Oasis Resort, Landsborough Pde, Golden Beach, tel: (07) 5491-0333, fax: 5491-0300. Fully serviced 1-, 2- and 3-bedroom luxury apartments makes this an ideal family resort, with the added attraction of a quality licensed restaurant.
Gemini Resort, Golden Beach, tel: (07) 5492-2200, fax: 5492-1000. 1- and 2-bedroom apartments situated right on the beach, 2 heated swimming pools, spas, tennis and an excellent licensed restaurant.

BUDGET
Anchorage Motor Inn and Resort, 18 Bowman Rd, tel: (07) 5491-1499, fax: 5491-7279. Reasonably priced resort offering 1- and 2-bedroom apartments close to shops and beaches.

Maroochydore
Chateau Royale, Memorial and Sixth Avenues, tel: (07) 5443-0300, fax: 5443-0371. Luxury beachfront resort with beach houses all facing north, each with its own balcony and spectacular views.
Novotel Twin Waters Resort, Ocean Dr, Mudjimba Beach, tel: (07) 5448-8000, fax: 5448-8001. North of Maroochydore, luxury resort set in 267ha (659 acres) of unspoilt bushland. Golf, windsurfing, canoeing and more.

BUDGET
Coachmans Court Motor Inn, 94 Sixth Ave, tel: (07) 5443-4099, fax: 5443-5876. Motel accommodation, centrally located for all activities.
Heritage Motor Inn, 69 Sixth Ave, tel: (07) 5443-7355, fax: 5443-3794. Well-appointed motel which is conveniently located.

Noosa Heads
Noosa has a large variety of accommodation from the very expensive to the inexpensive.
Noosa Tourist Information Centre, Hastings Street, tel: (07) 5447 4988. Provides advice on accommodation and services in the Noosa area.
Sheraton Noosa, Hasting Street, tel: (07) 5449-4888, fax: 5449-2230. Luxurious resort in the heart of Noosa.
No 1 in Hastings Street, cnr Hastings Street and Morwong Dr, tel: (07) 5449-2211, fax: 5449-2001. Elegant apartments and penthouses overlooking Noosa Beach.
Noosa Harbour Resort, Quamby Place, tel: (07) 5447-4500, fax: 5447-2151. On Noosa Harbour, self-contained luxury apartments with all the facilities of a larger resort.

BUDGET
Seahaven Beachfront Resort, 13 Hastings Street, tel: (07) 5447-3422, fax: 5447-5260. Self-contained apartments in the heart of Noosa overlooking the Pacific Ocean.

The Sunshine Coast at a Glance

Gympie

Situated on the Mary River, Gympie is the centre of a rich agricultural and pastoral region. The Gympie Show (May) and the Gympie Country Music Muster (August) are major events.

Great Eastern Motor Inn, 27 Geordie Rd, tel: (07) 5482-7288, fax: 5482-6445. Comfortable motel, some with kitchens, licensed restaurant.

Gympie Muster Inn, 21 Wickham Street, tel: (07) 5482-8666, fax: 5482-8601. Centrally located and well-appointed motel with salt water pool.

BUDGET

Golden Gate Motor Inn, Bruce Hwy, tel: (07) 5482-3611. This small motel is very well appointed and boasts a pool and BBQ area.

WHERE TO EAT

The Sunshine Coast has a wide range of restaurants.

Caloundra

St. Clairs on the Water, Golden Beach Resort, Golden Beach, tel: (07) 5437-4258. Excellent cuisine served in a delightful setting.

Deck Restaurant Oasis Resort, Landsborough Pde, tel: (07) 5491-0333. Quality restaurant attached to Norm Proven's Oasis Resort

Thai Suphan, cnr Bowman Rd and First Street, tel: (07) 5491-7899. Thai food served by a friendly staff.

Tivoli's Restaurant, 22 and 22a Bullock Street, tel: (07) 5491-1768. A wide assortment of fresh food served in this charming restaurant.

Maroochydore

Bullockies Steak and Seafood Restaurant, 80 Sixth Avenue, tel: (07) 5443-6665. Centrally located steak and seafood restaurant.

Rusty's Mexican Restaurant, 68 Sixth Street, tel: (07) 5443-1795. Popular Mexican restaurant in the heart of town.

Hathi Indian Restaurant, 14 Aerodrome Road, tel: (07) 5443-5411. Wide selection of Indian food.

Hoi Ting Inn, cnr Aerodrome Road and Sixth Avenue, tel: (07) 5443-1322. Chinese food served by friendly staff.

Noosa

Café Noosa, 1 David Low Way, tel: (07) 5447-3949. Italian food served al fresco seven days a week.

CoCo's, Laguna Bay, tel: (07) 5447-2440. The perfect dining experience overlooking the beautiful Laguna Bay.

Bistro C Beach Bar, Hastings Street, tel: (07) 5447-2855. Reasonably priced chargrill and bar on the beach.

Café Star, Hastings Street, tel: (07) 5474-9600. Fully licensed restaurant offering wonderful food and live jazz.

Gympie

The Park Gate, Mary Street, tel: (07) 5482-1506. Delightful atmosphere and quality steaks.

Geordies Licensed Restaurant, 27 Geordie Rd, tel: (07) 5482-7288. Exceptional food, pleasant atmosphere.

Areebas Mexican Cantina Bruce Highway, tel: (07) 5483-9300. Popular Mexican restaurant.

TOURS AND EXCURSIONS

Laguna Day Tours, tel toll free: 1800 114 434. Offers a range of day tours.

Everglades Cruises, tel: (07) 5449-7362. Enjoy the beautiful Noosa River and the everglades on this half day tour.

Noosa Hinterland Tours, tel: (07) 5474-3366. Explore the scenic hinterland.

Maroochy River Cruises, tel: (07) 5479-1711. Explore the Maroochy River.

USEFUL CONTACTS

Caloundra Information Centre, Caloundra Rd, tel: (07) 5491-0202.

Noosa Junction Tourist Information Centre, 5/20 Sunshine Beach Road, tel: (07) 5447-3798.

Gympie Tourist Information Centre, Bruce Highway, tel: (07) 5483-5444.

Queensland Parks and Wildlife Service:
Noosa – Park Rd, tel: (07) 5447-3243.
Gympie – Bruce Highway, tel: (07) 5482-4189.

6
The Central Coast

Queensland's central coast region is unlike the Sunshine or Gold coasts in that its major tourist attractions, **Fraser Island**, the **Whitsundays**, and its major cities of **Bundaberg**, **Rockhampton**, **Mackay** and **Townsville** are often separated by long stretches of uninteresting road which passes for hundreds of kilometres through scrubby, cattle country. There are points when the road is far from the coast and the traveller is hardly aware that to the east lies the southern section of the **Great Barrier Reef**. Despite the distances, this area is arguably the most interesting of coastal Queensland.

Fraser Island, the world's largest sand island, is a true wonder with freshwater lakes, cool inland rainforest and streams, mountainous dunes and impossibly white sands.

The trip out to the Great Barrier Reef through the Whitsunday Islands is about as close to true tropical paradise as any traveller could reasonably ask for. The opportunities to experience the coral formations of the reef and to watch the brightly coloured tropical fish as they dart through the coral are endless.

The area's towns and cities also have their own charm. Bundaberg, Rockhampton, Mackay and Townsville all have large numbers of handsome turn-of-the-century and late 19th-century buildings. They also have elegant parks – mostly located on rivers – and good swimming facilities where the traveller can cool off.

This is the area where the true tropics start. Rockhampton sits astride the Tropic of Capricorn and all points north experience tropical conditions.

DON'T MISS

*** Fraser Island: the world's largest sand island, a magic mixture of freshwater lakes, huge dunes and long flat beaches.
*** A Day Trip to the Outer Reef: the Whitsundays is a must for everyone visiting this region.
*** Townsville Castle Hill Lookout: a prominent pink granite monolith which towers some 286m (938ft) above the city.

Opposite: *Whitehaven Beach on the eastern side of Whitsunday Island is famous for its dazzling white quartz sand beach.*

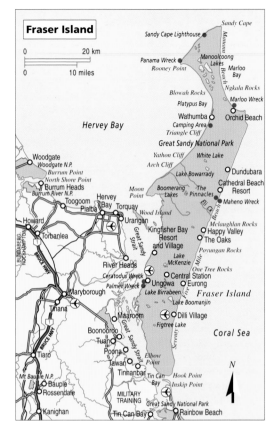

Fraser Island

| 0 | 20 km |
| 0 | 10 miles |

Sandy Cape
Sandy Cape Lighthouse
Panama Wreck
Rooney Point
Manooltoong Lakes
Marloo Bay
Ngkala Rocks
Blowah Rocks
Platypus Bay
Marloo Wreck
Wathumba
Orchid Beach
Camping Area
Triangle Cliff
Great Sandy National Park
Hervey Bay
Yathon Cliff
White Lake
Arch Cliff
Lake Bowarrady
Dundubara
Moon Point
Boomerang Lakes
The Pinnacles
Cathedral Beach Resort
Maheno Wreck
Woodgate
Woodgate N.P.
Burrum Point
North Shore Point
Burrum Heads
Burrum River N.P.
Toogoom
Pialba
Hervey Bay
Torquay
Wood Island
Urangan
Mclaughlan Rocks
Howard
Kingfisher Bay Resort and Village
Happy Valley
The Oaks
Torbanlea
Lake McKenzie
Poyungan Rocks
One Tree Rocks
River Heads
Ceratodus Wreck
Palmer Wreck
Ungowa
Eurong
Central Station
Maryborough
Lake Birrabeen
Fraser Island
Lake Boomanjin
Tiana
Maaroom
Dilli Village
Figtree Lake
Coral Sea
Boonooroo
Tuan
Poona
Tiaro
Tawan
Elbow Point
Mt Bauple N.P.
Tinnanbar
Tin Can Bay
Hook Point
Bauple
Inskip Point
Rossendale
MILITARY TRAINING
Great Sandy National Park
Kanighan
Tin Can Bay
Rainbow Beach

N

HERVEY BAY AND FRASER ISLAND

Most people travel to **Hervey Bay** to make the crossing to Fraser Island or to join a cruise out to see the whales. In recent times Hervey Bay has become an increasingly popular holiday destination. It is a loosely connected series of villages – **Urangan**, **Torquay**, **Scarness**, **Pialba** and **Point Vernon** – stretching along the bay and consisting of small shopping centres and a seemingly endless run of holiday units, motels, caravan parks and flats.

Hervey Bay's great attraction lies in its range of activities – whale spotting, fishing, walking, water skiing, scuba diving, and exploring nearby Fraser Island. There are also the usual tourist attractions of a wildlife park, a bird sanctuary and an aquarium. There is an interesting and substantial historical museum and a memorial to the kanakas (see p. 27) who worked the sugar fields in the area.

Fraser Island ★★★

Fraser Island lies just off the coast from Hervey Bay. It is 123km (76 miles) long and varies from 7km (4½ miles) to 22km (13½ miles) wide. Covering 184,000km² (71,024 sq miles) with sand dunes rising to a height of 240m (787ft) it is estimated that the sands which make up Fraser Island reach over 600m (373ft) below the sea.

Opposite above: *Hervey Bay's attractions include whale watching, visiting Fraser Island, the Shark Show, and meeting the seals at the Neptune Coral Cave.*
Opposite below: *Fraser Island scenery ranges from the cool rainforest at Central Station to the huge sand dunes on its eastern coast.*

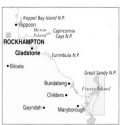

TOP ATTRACTIONS
OF FRASER ISLAND

The only way to travel around Fraser Island is by 4WD. Vehicles can be hired or there are a number of excellent conducted tours including one which starts from Kingfisher Bay Resort and includes the Stonetool sand dune (a huge, slowly moving dune), the tranquil waters of Eli Creek, the wreck of the Maheno, the Pinnacles and the Cathedrals, Central Station and Lake McKenzie. These are recognised as the major attractions on the island.

Eli Creek is an area of exceptional and pristine beauty with a number of wooden walkways. A short, circular route runs up one side of the creek and down the other. It is possible to swim in the lower reaches of the creek. The *Maheno* is the wreck of a cruise ship which came aground on Fraser Island in 1935. The **Pinnacles and the Cathedrals** are spectacular coloured sand cliffs of red, brown, yellow and orange. The size of the cliff faces is a reminder of how large the sand dunes on the island are. **Central Station** is in the centre of the island and the **Wanggoolba Creek** is one of the most beautiful retreats on the whole of the island.

*** **Eli Creek:** the largest freshwater stream on the eastern coast of the island.
*** **Central Station and Woongoolbver Creek:** carries clear water through the island's rainforest at Central Station.
*** **Fresh-water lakes:** include Lake Bowarrady, Lake McKenzie, Lake Boomanjin, Ocean Lake, Hidden Lake, and Coomboo Lake.
** **Wreck of the *Maheno*:** on the island's eastern beach.
** **Pinnacles and the Cathedrals:** coloured sand cliffs have been sculptured by the wind and rain blowing in off the Pacific Ocean.

BUNDABERG RUM

Bundaberg's greatest tourist attraction is the Bundaberg Rum distillery which is clearly signposted east of the city centre. There is a 40–50 minute conducted tour of the Distillery which leaves the Visitors Centre at 10:00, 11:00, 13:00, 14:00 and 15:00. Visitors observe the fermenting tanks, wash column, condensers, pot still, maturation vats and bottling but do not get free samples.

Opposite: *The Singing Ship sculpture at Emu Park sings almost constantly because of onshore breezes. The sculpture commemorates the 200th Anniversary of Cook's discovery of Australia.*
Below: *In the heart of sugar cane country, Bundaberg is famous for its 'Bundy' rum which is manufactured at the Bundaberg distillery east of the town.*

There are a number of freshwater lakes on the island including **Lake Bowarrady** (120m/394ft above sea level), **Lake McKenzie**, **Lake Boomanjin** (reputedly the largest perched lake in the world), **Ocean Lake**, **Hidden Lake**, and **Coomboo Lake.** Each is notable for the clarity of the water, the purity of the white sands on the surrounding beaches and the peacefulness of the area. They are ideal places for picnics.

BUNDABERG
Tropical parks and gardens, lazy green-brown tropical rivers, the heady scent of bougainvillea and jasmine are the characteristics of Bundaberg. Also to be enjoyed is the tour of the famous **Bundaberg Rum Distillery.**

Bundaberg has a superb **Botanic Gardens Complex** where the famous Australian aviator **Bert Hinkler's** English home is located.

Mystery Craters *
Beyond the Gardens are the **Mystery Craters** which have featured in the 'Unsolved Mysteries of the World' TV series. They are a strange collection of 35 craters that have baffled teams of international geologists. The craters can be viewed at close quarters and there is an observation platform which allows people to get an overview of the whole area. They are open from 08:00–17:00 seven days a week.

Mon Repos Environmental Park and Bangara ***
The park is a protected beach and foreshore area where (November–March) turtles come ashore to lay eggs.

Around **Mon Repos** and **Bargara** there is evidence of the work of the South Sea Islanders who came to Australia in the late 1800s as virtual slaves. Stone walls built by the kanakas can be seen on the southern side of Bargara Road near the edge of town and there are long walls on the road between Bargara and Mon Repos. **The Basin** at the very southern end of the Esplanade in Bargara has a sheltered swimming area built out of local volcanic rock by kanaka labour.

ROCKHAMPTON

Rockhampton is one of Queensland's most impressive cities. The buildings reflect the wealth resulting from the Mt Morgan's gold mines. Visitors should walk around the centre, particularly **Quay Street** and **East Street** where there is a concentration of beautiful old buildings, tree-lined streets and malls. The lazy Fitzroy River is on the northern side of Quay Street. The *Rockhampton's Heritage* brochure (available at the Tourist Information Centre in East Street Mall) lists 26 historical buildings.

Visitors may also drive south to the **Botanic Gardens** which boasts a range of tropical and warm climate plants. A separate Japanese Garden was established in 1982.

North of the city the attractions include the **Dreamtime Cultural Centre** on **Glenmore Homestead**. Glenmore Homestead is one of many interesting old buildings in the rural hinterland and a fine example of the primitive-style construction adopted by early settlers. Nearby is a slab house which was once a Bush Inn and a stone and adobe house built by a Mexican stone mason in 1862.

Olsens Capricorn Caves **

The 16 caves, 20km (12½ miles) out of town, were first discovered by John Olsen, a Norwegian migrant, in 1882. Formed from an ancient coral reef some 380 million years ago, the caves are privately owned and therefore are used for such unlikely activities as weddings and parties.

TOP ATTRACTIONS OF ROCKHAMPTON

*** The Historic buildings:** Quay and East streets.
** Botanic Gardens and Japanese Gardens:** excellent gardens, first developed in 1869.
** The Dreamtime Cultural Centre:** set in beautiful gardens, including a small waterfall and a pond; aims to introduce visitors to the culture of Central Queensland Aborigines and the peoples of the Torres Strait Islands.
** Glenmore Homestead:** classified by the National Trust, the Homestead complex consists of the original log cabin (1858).
** Olsens Capricorn Caves:** the oldest tourist attraction in Queensland.

Above: Shute Harbour is the major port in the Whitsundays. Each day cruises and yachts leave the harbour to explore the islands.

Towns close to Rockhampton worth visiting include **Emu Park** where visitors may get a fine view of the Pacific Ocean from the headland near the remarkable Singing Ship musical sculpture in Kele Park which sings almost constantly because of the on-shore breezes.

Further north is **Yeppoon** a holiday resort town which includes one of the first exclusive Japanese resorts on the Queensland coast.

Mount Morgan ***

One of Australia's finest 19th-century gold mining towns, **Mount Morgan** is steeped in the history of its golden days. Visits may be arranged but the most interesting attractions are the suspension bridges across the creek which were used by miners walking from town to the mine.

TOP ATTRACTIONS OF THE WHITSUNDAYS

*** A day trip to the Outer Reef: a superb introduction to the beauty of the region.
*** Scuba diving: near the fringing Reefs.
** Tropical rainforest: excellent walking tracks.
** The resorts: the major islands all have resorts; take your pick of Daydream Island, Dent Island, Hamilton Island, Hayman Island, Hook Island, Lindeman Island, Long Island, or South Molle Island.

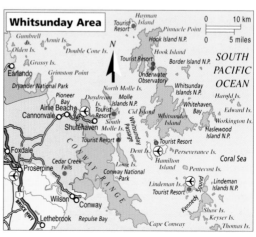

THE WHITSUNDAYS

Whitsunday encompasses a large 'town' which includes the mainland settlements of **Airlie Beach**, **Cannonvale** and **Shute Harbour**, the Whitsunday Islands and the reef which runs through the whole area.

Airlie Beach is the centre the Whitsunday group and is a myriad of gift shops, eateries ranging from fast foods to quality restaurants, pubs and bars, and shops catering for holidaymakers with a distinctly tropical flavour.

Shute Harbour is nothing more than a lot of parking spaces, a few motels and holiday homes and a harbour where the cruises and the ferries leave for the Whitsunday Islands. It is reputedly the second busiest harbour in Australia after Sydney's Circular Quay.

Whitsunday Islands ✶✶✶

The **Whitsunday Islands** are all 'drowned' mountains. They create a network of 74 islands of which only seven have resort facilities. The area beyond the resorts is part of the **Great Barrier Reef Marine Park** and the uninhabited islands are all controlled by National Parks and Wildlife.

The most accessible islands include **Daydream Island** which is sometimes called the 'Honeymooners Isle' because it is small and intimate compared to the large resorts on Hamilton and Hayman Islands, and **South Molle Island** which boasts facilities for over 600 guests and the usual range of activities from golf, tennis and squash to bushwalking, scuba diving, cycling and just lazing on the beaches.

It takes around two and a half hours to travel from Shute Harbour to the **Outer Reef Platform**, a large, permanent structure on the western side of Hardy Reef. The cruise usually spends three and a half hours at the platform

Below: *Recognised as one of the premier resorts in the Whitsunday group, Hamilton Island offers a wide variety of accommodation, excellent restaurants and a number of luxurious swimming pools.*

**WALKING ON
MAGNETIC ISLAND**

Magnetic Island is a delightful
island with over 20km (12½
miles) of walking tracks.
• **Nelly Bay to Arcadia:**
a 6km (4 mile) track.
• **The Hawkins Point Trail:**
exceptional views of Townsville.
• **The trail to the top
of Mount Cook.**
• **Arthur Bay and 'The
Forts':** a 1.4km (¾ mile)
long track.
• **Picnic Bay to West Point:**
8km (5 mile) walk along the
island's coastline.
• **Horseshoe Bay Lagoon:**
about 700m (230ft) long
which leads from Horseshoe
Bay Beach to the Lagoon
Environmental Park.

which is more than enough time snorkel, travel along the edge of the reef in the Reefworld sub (a semi-submersible vessel which allows visitors to sit in a large cabin underwater and watch as the sub passes over sections of coral at the edge of the reef), go swimming, visit the platform's underwater observatory and enjoy a smorgasbord lunch which is included in the price of the tour.

Perhaps the most spectacular way to see the reef (although it is not cheap) is to take a five- or 10-minute joy flight in a helicopter. The helipad is moored about 200m (656ft) from the platform and the number of joy flights is determined by the demand.

TOWNSVILLE

Townsville is a fascinating and gracious city which proudly calls itself 'The Tropical Capital of North Queensland'. It offers the visitor an opportunity to explore the district's historic past, travel across to Magnetic Island and climb the rocky outcrops and enjoy some truly outstanding lookouts and vantage points.

Townsville also has an excess of National Trust buildings and consequently it is a feast for those interested in impressive late 19th-century public architecture and classic north Queensland-style domestic and private architecture. The public buildings in the area of **Flinders Street** and **The Strand** create streetscapes of great elegance and beauty.

Below: *Located on the harbour at the end of the commercial district, the North Queensland Insurance Building, is typical of Townsville's impressive architecture.*

The **Tattersalls Hotel** at the bottom end of Flinders Street, a typical Australian hotel of its period, was built in 1865. It has wide upstairs verandahs and attractive iron balustrades.

The city's lookouts offer truly magnificent vantage points. The most popular and accessible is **Castle Hill**, a prominent pink granite monolith some

286m (938ft) above the city. The view at night is dramatic and during the day it is one of the eastern coast's finest viewpoints.

The climb to the top of **Mount Stuart** is rewarding. The road to the summit is located 2km (1½ miles) south of Townsville and the view, from 585m (1919ft) up, is quite spectacular.

Great Barrier Reef Aquarium ✱✱✱

Townsville is a city of great charm and has not been overwhelmed by tourism. The city's central attraction is the **Great Barrier Reef Aquarium**, a combination of museum, aquarium, departure point to Magnetic Island and large screen Omnimax theatre. It has the only living coral reef in captivity – which means that visitors can actually see the Great Barrier Reef while safely on land.

Above: *Magnetic Island, located just off the coast from Townsville, has over 20km (1½ miles) of walking tracks and is ideal for bushwalkers and backpackers.*

Magnetic Island ✱✱✱

Be sure to take a ferry trip across to **Magnetic Island**, a delightful island with over 20km (12½ miles) of walking tracks. Nearly half the island is taken up by the **Magnetic Island National Park**, offering an opportunity to view the island's wildlife and to explore its bushland.

The island's eastern side has four small settlements at **Horseshoe Bay** (the island's major residential area), **Arcadia**, **Nelly Bay** and **Picnic Bay.** Some 2533ha (6257 acres) of the central area and western side of the island is now national park with six established walking trails.

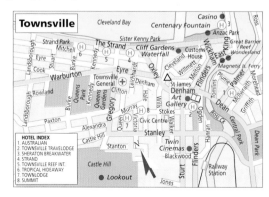

The Central Coast at a Glance

Summer temperatures hover between 25°C–30°C (77°F–86°F) with warm nights, (**December** to **February**). This is the 'wet' season. **March** to **November** offers the best weather with clear sunny days and mild evenings. Whale watching in Hervey Bay is a major attraction between August and October.

GETTING THERE

Hervey Bay
Hervey Bay is a short flight from Brisbane by **Sunstate Airlines**, tel: 13 1313. The airline has a daily service. Taxis and a shuttle bus service will take you into the town. Larger resorts will arrange to meet the plane. Major coach companies offer regular services from Brisbane; the trip takes about 4½ hours. **Greyhound/Pioneer**, tel: 13 2030 and **McCafferty's**, tel: 13 1499.

Bundaberg, Rockhampton and Airlie Beach
Rail service to area is 'The **Capricornian**', Friday and Sunday, 'The **Sunlander**' on Tuesday, Thursday and Saturday, tel: 132 232. **Greyhound/Pioneer** and **McCafferty's** have daily services from Brisbane. **Sunstate** has a daily flight out of Brisbane. Fraser Island is accessible only by ferry. They depart regularly from **Urangan Boat Harbour**. Central booking office, tel: (07) 4125-4444. The Bruce Highway is an inland road. It doesn't join the coast until Gladstone. Bundaberg is 51km (31½ miles) east of the Highway and Airlie Beach is 24km (15 miles) from Proserpine.

GETTING AROUND

Maryborough–Hervey Bay Coaches, tel: (07) 4121-3719, run a service between the two centres several times a day Monday to Friday. Car rentals, particularly 4WD, are the favoured mode of transport. A visit to the local Tourist Information Centre is advisable. Airlie Beach has a local bus service as well as taxis.

WHERE TO STAY

Hervey Bay
Hervey Bay Resort, 249 Esplanade, Pialba, tel: (07) 4128-1555. Comfortable motel. **Delfinos Bay Resort**, 383 Esplanade, Torquay, tel: (07) 4124-1666. Serviced apartments.

BUDGET
Fairway Motel, 29 Boat Harbour Drive, Pialba, tel: (07) 4128-1911. Small, comfortable, reasonably priced motel. **Golden Sands Motor Inn**, 44 Main Street, Pialba, tel: (07) 4128 3977. Well-located motel.

Fraser Island
Kingfisher Bay Resort, North White Cliffs, tel: (07) 4120-3333 or toll free 1800 072 555, fax: (07) 4127-9333. The ultimate in resort living.

BUDGET
Fraser Island Retreat, East Coast, tel: (07) 4127-9144, fax: 4127-9131. Comfortable, well-equipped bungalows. Perfect location on the east coast. **National Parks and Wildlife**, Maryborough Office, tel: (07) 4121-1800. Many beautiful camping areas. Booking and information from the National Parks and Wildlife.

Bundaberg
Bundaberg international Motor Inn, 73 Takalvan Street, tel: (07) 4151-2365, fax: 4153-1866. Well-appointed, central. **Reef Gateway Motor Inn**, 11 Takalvan Street, tel: (07) 4153-2255, fax: 4153-2294. Well-located motel offering a high standard of service.

BUDGET
Acacia Motor Inn, 248 Bourbong Street, tel: (07) 4152-3411, fax: 522-2387. Reasonable priced, central. **Bundaberg Spanish Motor Inn**, 134 Woongarra Street, tel: (07) 4152-5444, fax: 4152-5970. Quiet location, pool.

Rockhampton
Country Comfort Inn, 86 Victoria Pde, tel: (07) 4927-9933, toll free 008 023 962 fax: 4927-1615. All the facilities of a big city motel. **Centre Point Motor Inn**, 131 George Street, tel: (07) 4927-8844, fax: 4927-8732. Conveniently located motel with all the modern amenities.

The Central Coast at a Glance

BUDGET
Country Lodge Motor Inn,
112 Gladstone Rd, tel: (07)
4927-8866, fax: 4927-9711.
Comfortable, reasonable price.

Airlie Beach
Club Crocodile Whitsunday,
Shute Harbour Rd, tel: (07)
4946-7155, toll free 1800 075
151 fax: (07) 4946-6007.
Resort with bar, bistro, 2 pools.
**Whitsunday Terrace and
Village Resorts**, Golden Orchid
Drive, tel: (07) 4946-6788,
fax: 4946-7128. Self-contained;
suit couples or families.

BUDGET
Airlie Court, 382 Shute
Harbour Rd, tel: (07) 4946-
6218. Well-appointed units.

Townsville
**Sheraton Townsville Hotel
and Casino**, Sir Leslie Thiess
Drive, tel: (07) 4722-2333, fax:
4722-3488. Luxury; marina.
Seagulls Resort, 74 The
Esplanade, toll free: 1800 079
929, fax: (07) 4721-3133.
Award-winning seaside resort.

BUDGET
Ridgemont Executive Motel,
15 Victoria Street, toll free:
1800 804 168, fax: (07) 4772-
1270. In the heart of Townsville.

WHERE TO EAT

Hervey Bay
Melanesia Village, 49–63
Elizabeth Street, Urangan, tel:
(07) 4128-9702. Dining and
entertainment extravaganza.

Don Camillo, The Esplanade,
Torquay, tel: (07) 4128-1087.
Traditional Italian cuisine.

Fraser Island
The Sand Bar, Kingfisher Bay
Village, tel: (07) 4120-3333.
Bar, bistro and pizzeria.
Maheno Restaurant, King-
fisher Bay Resort, tel: (07)
4120-3333. Great restaurant
offering buffet, theme dinners.

Bundaberg
Christina's BYO Restaurant,
238 Bourbong Street, tel: (07)
4153-1770. Australian, Greek
cuisine.
Charley Magees, 61 Perry
Street, tel: (07) 4153-1553.
Reasonably priced restaurant.

Rockhampton
Hogs Breath Café, Aquatic
Place, tel: (07) 4926-3646.
Fun family restaurant.

Airlie Beach
**Mangroves Restaurant and
Swamp Bistro**, Club Crocodile,
(07) 4946-7155. A la carte or
a casual indoor/outdoor Bistro.
**The Palms Licensed Restaur-
ant**, Colonial Palms Motor Inn,
tel: (07) 4946-7166. Elegant,
breathtaking harbour views.

Townsville
**The Pier Waterfront Restaur-
ant and Bar**, Sir Leslie Thiess
Drive, tel: (07) 4721-2567.
Exeptional food, great location
Sirocca Café Bar and Grill,
61 Palmer St, tel: (07) 4724-
4508. East meets west.

TOURS AND EXCURSIONS

**Kingfisher Bay Resort
Tours**, Fraser Island,
tel: (07) 4120-3333. 4WD
tours of Island visiting all the
beauty spots. Whale watch
cruises in season.
Bundaberg Distillery Tour,
Bundaberg, tel: (07) 4150-
8684. Tours daily 10:00–15:00.
Rothery Coaches, tel: (07)
4922-4320. Guided day tours
of the Rockhampton area.
FantaSea Cruises, Shute
Harbour, tel: (07) 4946-5111.
Explore the Great Barrier Reef.
Detours Coaches, Shop 5
Barrier Reef Wonderland,
tel: (07) 4771-3986. Day tours
around Townsville
**Hervey Bay Information
Centre**, 333 The Esplanade,
Scarness, tel: (07) 4124-6911.

USEFUL CONTACTS

**Queensland National Parks
and Wildlife**, Bundaberg
Office, Govt. Office Bld, Quay
St, tel: (07) 4131-1600.
**Bundaberg Tourist Infor-
mation Centre**, Bourbong
Street, tel: (07) 4152-2333.
**Whale Watch Tourist
Centre**, Shop 1 Hervey Bay
Marina, Urangan, toll free:
1800 358 595.
**Townsville Information
Centre**, Flinders Mall, tel:
(07) 4721-3660.
**Fraser Coast Holiday
Centre**, Esplanade, Hervey
Bay, tel: (07) 4124-9685.
**Rockhampton Tourist Infor-
mation Centre**, Quay Street,
tel: (07) 4922-5339.

7
The Far North

To the west and north of Cairns lies the Far North of Queensland – a region characterised by tropical rainforest along the coast, dry inland areas, old mining towns and one of the richest concentrations of flora and fauna anywhere in Australia. This is an area of vast distances, few towns – **Mossman**, **Port Douglas**, **Weipa**, **Cooktown** – and tiny settlements like **Bamaga** on the tip of Cape York.

The southern end of the region – which includes **Cairns**, **Kuranda** and the beaches from Cairns to **Port Douglas** – is the major tourist area. In winter there are numerous daily tours out to the **Great Barrier Reef** and the train and **Skyrail** run thousands of visitors to the pleasant mountain village of Kuranda. In summer tourism declines because of the often cyclonic weather conditions (the region's rainfall is concentrated in the summer months) and the presence of the deadly box jellyfish along the coast. This is a winter holiday area.

Beyond the coast are the **Atherton Tablelands**. These rich and fertile tablelands sustain a range of crops as well as a substantial dairy and beef industry. The area's dairy products are recognised as some of the finest in Australia.

The Far North is a combination of high-level tourism and adventure holidays. Beyond the main centres the roads become unreliable and 4WD vehicles a necessity.

The area has developed dramatically over the past 20 years due to the construction of an international airport at Cairns. This resulted in a building boom. It is also now a popular destination for backpackers and Japanese tourists.

DON'T MISS

*** Kuranda Railway: across waterfalls and through rainforests.
*** Skyrail: rare opportunity to see rainforests from above.
*** Tjapukai Cultural Theme Park: unique experience of Aboriginal culture.
*** Cape Tribulation: unspoilt tropical rainforest.
*** Outer Reef: take an inspiring cruise tour.

Opposite: *Queensland's far north is noted for its pristine rainforests and wilderness areas which are characterised by waterfalls, mountain streams and spectacular views to the coast.*

Right: *Cruises to the Great Barrier Reef and Green Island leave from the pier area of Cairns harbour. The marina is home to the sailors who spend their winter in the Cairns district.*

CAIRNS

Cairns is the major city in the Far North. Although the city has no beaches of its own, it lies at the centre of an area that is truly a tropical paradise: to the north of the city are palm-fringed beaches; to the east spectacular rainforests, exotic fauna and flora and dramatic waterfalls; to the west the islands, reefs and coral cays of the Great Barrier Reef.

In 1984 Cairns airport was upgraded to international standard making travelling to the region a lot easier.

Historic Cairns ★★

The most interesting buildings in town are in the Wharf Road, Abbott Street and Lake Street areas. Here is the famous 'Barbary Coast' collection of buildings, most

vividly seen in the two hotels – the Barrier Reef and Oceanic located on Wharf Street. This collection of buildings recalls the shipping origins of Cairns. Their location so close to the wharves and their wide verandahs and awnings extending over the footpaths make them an important part of Cairns' streetscape.

Kuranda Railway ★★

Apart from the ever-popular trips out to the Great Barrier Reef and Green Island, one of the major attractions in the Cairns area is the **Kuranda Railway**. It is probably the most scenically beautiful rail journey in Australia with one section actually crossing the face of the Stony Creek Falls and another zig-zagging the hillside and through no fewer than 15 tunnels. There are stunning views back across the Coral Sea. It was built by John Robb between 1886 and 1891 and is a masterpiece of railway engineering. In 1915 the Railway Station at Kuranda was completed. The highlight of the trip is the **Barron Falls**, which are only a short distance from **Kuranda Railway Station**, famous for its beautiful tropical gardens.

Opposite below: *Famous for its superb tropical gardens, Kuranda Railway Station is the end of the most beautiful and spectacular railway journey in tropical Queensland.*

Tjapukai Cultural Theme Park ★★★

The theme park, next to the Caravonica Lakes Station in north Cairns, is a unique attempt to explain Aboriginal culture in a broad thematic way. It offers visitors a rare opportunity to experience Aboriginal culture through a Cultural Village, a Creation Theatre (in which the story of creation is told in the Tjapukai language – with headset translations), a History Theatre (an overview of Aboriginal history in the past 120 years) and Magic Space with giant murals. Visitors to the theme park can experience all the performances over a 2-hour period.

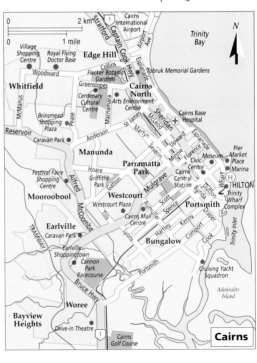

Right: *Leaving Cairns each day the train to Kuranda rises up the steep hinterland slopes crossing waterfalls, winding through rainforest and passing through narrow tunnels.*

Skyrail **

Also from here the **Skyrail** starts its spectacular 7.5km (4½ mile) journey over rainforest to Kuranda. It is one of Australia's most memorable tourist experiences.

The journey breaks at **Red Peak Station**, where it is possible to inspect the diversity of the rainforest from a wooden walkway, and at the **Barron Falls Station** for a glorious panorama of the Barron Gorge. Nowhere else on earth can you travel across a tropical river, beside a huge waterfall and across untouched tropical rainforest and experience the beauty without damaging the landscape.

KURANDA

At the end of the line is the tropical town of Kuranda which nestles on the edges of the rainforests and marks the entrance to the Atherton Tableland. Kuranda is awash with shops and activities including arts and craft shops; a seemingly endless selection of eateries from pie shops to coffee lounges and restaurants; and a market where candles, jewellery, leather goods, T–shirts, tropical fruits and woodwork are sold.

The town's three major tourist attractions are the **Noctarium**, where visitors can watch the night time activities of rainforest animals, a **Butterfly Sanctuary**, where some of the rainforests most beautiful and rare species of butterflies are on display, and the **markets** which are deservedly popular.

THE ATHERTON TABLELANDS

The Atherton Tablelands is an area of rich tropical rain-forests, fertile cattle country and undulating highlands. The tablelands were originally settled by gold prospectors and cattle men who discovered rich deposits and excellent pastures on these tropical highlands.

The largest town on the Atherton Tablelands is **Mareeba**, a service town with bright displays of flowers and flowering trees which adorn the central island in the town's main street. Mareeba's main attraction is the **Granite Gorge** with huge Granite Boulders which were formed by relatively recent volcanic activity.

The township of Atherton is another service centre. Of interest are the **Old Post Office Gallery**, now a gallery and museum, and the **Chinese Temple to the Emperor Ho Wong**, a rare combination of traditional Chinese architecture and local corrugated iron. The prominent local Fong On family are currently rebuilding the old temple and its adjacent kitchen annexe and community hall.

Yungaburra **

The most attractive of the townships on the tablelands, **Yungaburra** has many interesting buildings all built from local timber. No fewer than 23 have been listed by the National Trust. Yungaburra's great tourist attraction is the famous **Curtain Fig Tree** which is only 3km (2 miles) from the town on the Malanda Road. This huge tree has, by an accident of nature, created a curtain of roots dropping some 15m (49ft) from the main body of the tree to the ground. To the east of the town is **Lake Eacham** a huge crater lake which was probably formed as recently as 10,000 years ago. The walks around its foreshores are quite superb and the swimming facilities are excellent.

TOP ATTRACTIONS OF THE ATHERTON TABLELANDS

*** **Yungaburra:** attractive and historic township in the heart of the tablelands.
*** **Curtain and Cathedral Fig Trees:** impressive trees in the rainforest with remarkable hanging root systems.
** **Granite Gorge, Mareeba:** huge granite boulders have slumped across the landscape like Dali watches.
* **Halloran's Hill Environmental Park, Atherton:** crater of an extinct volcano.

Below: *The Atherton Tablelands is ideal for dairy and beef cattle. In recent times tobacco has become a major crop near the town of Mareeba.*

West of Yungaburra are **Tinaroo, Tinaroo Falls, Tinaroo Falls Dam** and **Lake Tinaroo. Tinaroo** is an ideal place to stay while exploring the 31km (19 mile) **Danbulla Forest Road**, which winds through a variety of vegetational zones of rainforests, where the spectacular **Cathedral Fig Tree** can be seen. There is also the beautiful crater **Lake Euramoo**, a popular haunt for bird watchers and ideal for a bushwalk.

The Falls off the Tableland **

The town of **Tinaroo Falls** has grown over the years and offers an escape from the heat of the coast. Its setting on the shores of the artificial lake is really beautiful. There's a peaceful caravan park nestled in the trees and there are facilities for boating and windsurfing on the lake.

Above: *Waterfalls abound on the Atherton Tablelands. 'The Waterfalls Circuit', a circular trip of less than one hour, includes the Millaa Millaa (pictured here), Zillie and Ellinjaa falls. There are at least five more sets of falls within the area.*

Opposite: *The road from the coastal sugar town of Gordonvale to the Atherton Tablelands offers many fine panoramic views as it winds through extensive areas of dense rainforest.*

Other falls worth visiting are the small ones on the outskirts of Malanda and the **Millaa Millaa Falls** which are located just a couple of kilometres out of town. Visitors can relax in their cars and watch the waterfalls. These falls are the first of a series of three falls on what is commonly known as 'The Waterfalls Circuit', a circular trip which encompasses the **Zillie Falls** and the **Ellinjaa Falls**. There are at least five more sets of falls within the area.

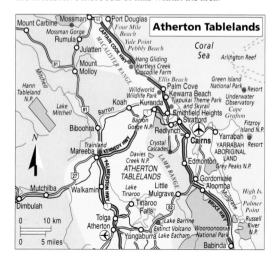

SOUTH OF CAIRNS

Travelling down the coast from Cairns the visitor passes through seemingly endless fields of sugar cane. To the west the Great Dividing Range rises from the flat coastal plain. This is an area of high rainfall and small sugar towns.

A few kilometres south is the tiny settlement (almost a suburb now) of Edmonton with a theme park, **Sugarworld**, which includes **Hambledon Sugar Mill** as part of its attractions. It also has a small exotic fruits orchard, a water slide, a restaurant and a special train which runs around the perimeter of the leisure park.

A further 9km (5½ miles) south is **Gordonvale**, which lays claim to the rather dubious privilege of being the place where the dreaded cane toad was first introduced to Australia. Behind the town stands 'The Pyramid' or Pyramid Hill, a volcanic core where a competition to see who can get to the top in the shortest time is run every year. The record currently stands at 1 hour 20 minutes. Close by **The Mulgrave Rambler**, a steam-driven sugar train, takes passengers across the Mulgrave River and through sections of rainforest before reaching the Orchid Valley, a substantial orchid nursery.

Further south, and west of the town of Babinda, are **The Boulders**, a series of large, dramatic rocks in the river which have been worn smooth by tropical rains.

Innisfail is home to a **Chinese Temple**, a reminder of the goldfields of North Queensland which attracted considerable numbers of Chinese who dispersed south to towns like Innisfail after the goldrushes.

Etty Bay and **Mission Beach** are delightful and unspoilt beaches. Mission Beach is one of the last

RAINFALL AT TULLY

Tully is known as Australia's wettest town. One year it had rainfall of 4267mm (168in). The annual average rainfall is 2127mm (84in). The town's location at the edge of the Great Dividing Range ensures that onshore breezes push rain-laden clouds onto the mountain range. This, combined with the cyclonic nature of the entire Far North, ensures that Tully records huge rainfalls. It also ensures that the nearby Tully Falls and Wallaman Falls are some of the most impressive falls in the country.

Above: *The Victoria Mill at Ingham crushes and processes the sugar cane from the surrounding farms. Regular inspections of the mill are organised through the local tourist information office.*

areas on the north Queensland coast where tropical rainforest actually reaches down to the shoreline.

Tully Falls ★★★

At Tully are the famous **Tully Falls** which can only be seen by entering the Tully Gorge National Park via Ravenshoe on the Atherton Tablelands. The river, only 115km (71 miles) long, drops dramatically off the escarpment and consequently has become a favourite place for white water rafting.

The flat lands between the coast and the mountains near **Ingham** are crisscrossed with narrow gauge tramways which bring sugar into the crushing mills. **Victoria Mill** is open for inspection during the crushing season.

Nearby is a remarkable **Italian cemetery** which looks like a city with its elaborate family mausoleums. The first Italians arrived in Ingham in 1891 and they were followed by continuous immigration between 1900–19. Another major period of immigration occurred between the wars. It is a fascinating insight into the lives of those who settled in this district.

**TOP ATTRACTIONS
SOUTH OF CAIRNS**

★★ **Sugarworld:** theme park with a sugar mill, orchard, water slide, restaurant and train.
★★ **Mulgrave Rambler:** steam-driven train that travels over the Mulgrave River and through a rainforest.
★★ **Chinese Temple:** located at Innisfail.
★★ **Etty Bay and Misson Beach:** delightful and unspoilt beaches.
★★ **Italian cemetery:** in Ingham with elaborate family mausoleums.

NORTH OF CAIRNS

To the north of Cairns lies the beautiful, diverse and relatively unspoilt region of the Daintree, Cape Tribulation and Cape York.

Port Douglas **

The Captain Cook Highway provides a unique and scenic route to Port Douglas as it is one of the few roads in Australia that actually runs close to the coastline. Port Douglas itself is pretty and tree-lined with a **Sheraton Mirage** resort and a chic shopping centre.

From here the road stretches north through fields of sugar cane before reaching the sugar mill town of **Mossman**. An alternative route would be the **Bally Hooley Rail Tour**. Each day at 9:00 an old steam train with open carriages leaves Port Douglas and travels across to Mossman where passengers can inspect the **Mossman Central Mill**.

Daintree National Park **

Mossman Gorge is at the southern end of the dense tropical rainforest of the **Daintree National Park**; home to Bennett's tree kangaroo, the cassowary, the Cairns birdwing butterfly and the giant atlas moth.

Travelling north, east of the Daintree National Park, you come to the tiny township of **Daintree**, the

Opposite below: *Cruises on the Daintree River are a rare opportunity to see estuarine crocodiles and inspect the rainforest which rises densely from the river banks.*

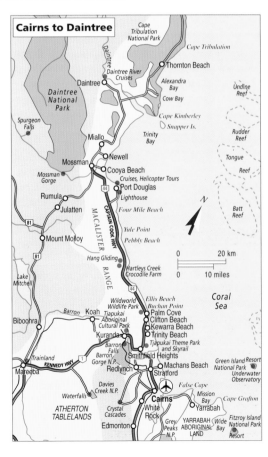

DAINTREE ATTRACTIONS

Daintree is a tiny township on the edge of the Daintree Rainforest. It offers:
** Daintree Rainforest River Trains: ecologically designed trip along the Daintree River.
** Daintree Timber Museum: insight into the timber cutters who first settled the area.
** Daintree Eco Centre: bird and butterfly enclosure and rainforest board walk.
** Rainforest Walks and Tours: number of tour operators offer walks and tours through the rainforest.

beginning of the northern wilderness. There are cruises down the river on the **M. V. *Spirit of Daintree*** which offers visitors an opportunity to see crocodiles as well as have a close inspection of the mangroves and the rainforest which edge the river.

Cape Tribulation National Park ***
Access to the beautiful **Cape Tribulation National Park** is by barge only and definitely with a 4WD. The sealed road ends at Daintree.

This is an area of breathtaking beauty with rugged mountain ranges rising sharply behind the narrow coastal strip, dense rainforest tumbling down the mountains to the beaches, and a bewilderingly rich variety of flora. The rainforest boasts extremely ancient species of fern which have been on earth for over 100 million years.

Captain Cook unceremoniously named the cape when his ship, the *Endeavour*, was damaged on a reef in 1770.

The Coast Road
The coastal road to Cooktown, particularly the section at the **Bloomfield River**, may well have the honour of the worst, or most challenging, road in Australia: unbelievable gradients, narrowness, bulldust, cavernous holes in the dry season and quagmires of mud in the wet. It has already caused considerable defilement of the environment. Conservationists have argued that the ecology of the area is so delicate that any development will automatically endanger the ecosystem. The road is not passable when there has been any rain and, even in good weather, the steepness of some of the slopes, the need to cross rivers at low tide, and the difficulty of the terrain mean that it is restricted to 4WD vehicles.

Below: *Cape Tribulation is the northernmost coastal point for conventional vehicles travelling from Cairns.*

COOKTOWN

The journey to Cooktown is long and difficult but worth the trip. This is where James Cook and his crew berthed on the river's edge to repair their boat. The town has no fewer than six monuments to Captain Cook – including a cairn at the place where he beached the *Endeavour*, another smaller monument a few metres away, a Bicentennial statue in a nearby park, and a huge civic monument further down the road. The town's lighthouse is also dedicated to Captain Cook.

Above: *The Black Mountain National Park, 28km (17 miles) south of Cooktown, has a strange mountain of huge granite boulders blackened by lichens.*

James Cook Historical Museum ★★

The **James Cook Historical Museum** (built in 1886) is a magnificent two-storey building, originally St Mary's Convent, constructed in the belief that the town would become a great centre in Australia. The Museum's exhibits include a recreated Chinese joss house (brought out from Canton), artefacts from the *Endeavour*, a shell collection and lots of material on Cooktown's early history.

Outside the town is **Black Mountain** a strange mountain of huge granite boulders blackened by lichens which form on the surface.

To the Cape

The road to **Bamaga**, just south of Cape York, is a difficult dirt road which crosses many rivers and is over 900km (560 miles) long. This is not a trip for the inexperienced and unprepared. A 4WD is the only vehicle for such terrain. The weather is hot and sticky, so plenty of fresh water is needed. The rivers are home to crocodiles.

The only industry of any importance began in 1955 when the Presbyterian mission of **Weipa** was found to contain the largest bauxite deposit in the world.

Much of Cape York, because of the poor access roads and the inhospitable terrain, has remained untouched.

ROAD TO CAPE YORK

The journey from Port Douglas to the tip of Cape York is one of Australia's great 4WD adventures. **Bamaga**, the last township before Cape York, is the most northern township in Queensland located some 61km (38 miles) north of the **Jardine River** and 983km (610 miles) north of Cairns. The journey, particularly from **Laura** onwards, is over difficult dirt road and across rivers. It is estimated that as many as 1000 4WD enthusiasts make the journey each year. It can only be made in winter as the summer rains make the journey impossible.

The Far North at a Glance

This area is known as the wet tropics. The 'wet' season is from mid December until the end of February. The best time to visit is **June**, **July** and **August**. The winter months are characterised by warm sunny days and mild evenings.

The far north is well serviced by all forms of transport. Cairns has an international airport. There are regular overseas and domestic flights. **Sunstate Airline** flies from Brisbane daily. tel: 13 1313. **Ansett**, tel: 131 300 and **Qantas**, tel: 131 313 also have regular services. The two major coach companies **Greyhound/ Pioneer**, tel: 13 2030 and **McCafferty's**, tel: 13 1499 offer regular services. The **Queenslander** train travels north every Sunday and offers first class only, which includes airconditioning and an excellent dining car. The **Sunlander** operates 3 times a week, Tuesday, Thursday and Saturday. For further information, tel: 13 2232. The Bruce Highway is the main road to Cairns.

There is an efficient bus shuttle service at Cairns Airport which travels to most of the major hotels. Contact (07) 4031-3555 or check at the airport information desk.

Coral Coaches operate a service which connects Cairns Airport to most major centres. It travels as far north as Cape Tribulation; tel: (07) 4031-7577. **Cairns City Airporter**, tel: (07) 4031-3555, run a bus service within the city. Car rental companies are plentiful in the major areas and are reasonably priced. Check at the Airport information counter or hotel/motel desk.

Cairns and the beaches north of the city have hundreds of hotels, motels and apartments. **Far North Queensland Promotion Bureau** puts out an informative magazine. **Cairns Hilton**, Wharf Street, toll free 1 800 222 255, fax: (07) 4050-2001. Centrally located, every luxury offered with magnificent views over Trinity Bay. **Cairns International**, 17 Abbott Street, tel: (07) 4031-1300, fax: 4031-1801. Hotel in the heart of the city with all the features of the larger resorts. **Radisson Plaza**, Pierpoint Rd, toll free 1 800 333 333, fax: (07) 4031-3226. Set in a tropical rainforest garden overlooking the Cairns inlet. **Mercure Hotel Harbourside**, 209–217 the Esplanade, toll free 1 800 642 244, fax: (07) 4051-0317. Situated on the harbour with the facilities of a bigger resort.

BUDGET
Cairns Tropical Gardens, 312–316 Mulgrave Rd, tel: (07) 4031-1777, fax: 4031-2605. Comfortable motel and apartment accommodation offering two pools, a spa and sauna.

Trinity Beach
Trinity Beach is 15km (9 miles) north from Cairns with an excellent swimming beach and facilities.
Costa Royal, 59–61 Vasey Esplanade, tel: 1800 805 708, fax (07) 4057-6577. On the beach, luxury fully serviced apartments or townhouses. **On the Beach**, 49–51 Vasey Esplanade, toll free 1800 627 878, fax: (07) 4057-7622. Fully serviced self-contained apartments beautifully appointed with balconies right on the beach.

Atherton Tablelands
Curtain Fig Motel, Gillies Highway, Yungaburra, tel: (07) 4095-3168, fax: 4095-2099. In the village, only 3km (2 miles) from the famous fig tree. **Chambers Wildlife Rainforest Apartments**, Eacham Close, Lake Eacham, tel: (07) 4095-3754. In the heart of the rainforest.

Port Douglas
Port Douglas Quest Resort, Port Douglas Rd, toll free 1800 334 033, fax: (07) 4099-4766. Luxury resort – popular with the family.

The Far North at a Glance

Sheraton Mirage, Port Douglas Rd, tel: (07) 4099-5888, fax: 4098-5885. Situated on Four Mile Beach this luxury resort has its very own golf course and extensive gardens.
Radisson Reef Resort, Port Douglas Rd, tel: (07) 4099-5577, fax 4099-5559. Self- contained townhouses with a wide range of facilities.

BUDGET
Port Douglas Outrigger, 16 Mudlo Street, tel: (07) 4099- 5662, fax: 4099-5717. Fully self-contained apartments, with a swimming pool and all the modern facilities; centrally located.
Garrick House, 11–13 Garrick Street, tel: (07) 4099-5322, fax: 4099-5021. Self-contained units with balconies or patios, fully serviced.

Cooktown
River of Gold Motel, cnr Hope and Walker streets, tel: (07) 4069-5222, fax: 4069-5615. Well-located motel with airconditioning and a swimming pool.
Sovereign Resort Hotel, Charlotte Street, tel: (07) 4069-5400, fax: 4069-5582. Large swimming pool with landscaped gardens and balcony restaurant.

WHERE TO EAT

Cairns
Damari's, 171 Lake Street, tel: (07) 4031-2155. Italian and seafood cuisine.

Kani's, 59 The Esplanade, tel: (07) 4051-1550. Seafood restaurant with superb views of Cairns.
Sushi Express Cairns, Orchid Plaza, tel: (07) 4041-4381. Fun Japanese cuisine, food on a train.
Red Ochre, 43 Shields Street, tel: (07) 4051-0100. The true taste of Australia, using Aboriginal foods to enhance this unique cuisine.

Atherton Tablelands
Nick's, Gillies Highway, Yungaburra, tel: (07) 4095-3330. Swiss/Italian cooking in a relaxed atmosphere.
Peeramon Historic Pub, Malanda Rd, Malanda, tel: (07) 4096-5873. Beautiful old pub with panoramic views.

Port Douglas
Catalina Restaurant, Wharf Street, tel: (07) 4099-5287. Popular local restaurant.
Chief's Mexican Restaurant, Macrossan Street, tel: (07) 4099-4199. A taste of Old Mexico.
Nautilus Restaurant, Murphy Street, tel: (07) 4099-5330. Excellent food served by friendly staff.
Wispers Restaurant, 20 Langley Road, tel: (070) 4099-3877. Fine dining in a quiet understated atmosphere.

Cooktown
River of Gold Motel Restaurant, Hope Street,

tel: (07) 4096-5222. Fully licensed restaurant in the motel complex.

TOURS AND EXCURSIONS

Jungle River Adventure, 7 Villa Street, Cairns, tel: (07) 4054-2552. 4km (2½ miles) of waterway in the tropical north.
Down Under Tours, Redden Street, tel: (07) 4035-5566. Coach tours to most of the popular spots including Undarra Lava Flows.
Skyrail, Cook Highway, Cairns, tel: (07) 4038-1555. The longest gondola cableway in the world travels over spectacular rainforest to Kuranda.
Aristocrat Reef Cruises, Port Douglas Marina Mirage, tel: (07) 4099-4727. **Captain Cook Tours**, Trinity Wharf, Cairns, tel: (07) 4031-4433. Daytrips to coral cays and the Outer Reef.

USEFUL CONTACTS

Cairns Tourist Information Centre, cnr Esplanade and Shield Streets, tel: (07) 4031-1715.
Port Douglas Information Centre, 23 Macrossan Street, tel: (07) 4099-5599.
Cooktown Tourist Information Centre, Biard Road, tel: (07) 4069-5755.
Queensland National Parks and Wildlife Service, 10–12 McLeod Street, Cairns, tel: (07) 4049-6600.

8
The Gulf Country

The Gulf Country, the Gulf Savannah and 'The Outback by the Sea' are names which have been given to that part of Queensland bounded by the Great Dividing Range and the Atherton Tablelands to the east, the Northern Territory to the west, and the Gulf of Carpentaria to the north. In the minds of most Australians this is a wilderness of mangrove swamps with a summer monsoon season when temperatures climb into the 40s (over 104°F), the humidity is unbearable and the heavy monsoonal rains fall with monotonous regularity.

But the Gulf is more than a dangerous wilderness. It is home to Queensland's lucrative barramundi industry and is rich in minerals. It was once the centre of an important gold-mining industry and gems like topaz, garnets and aquamarines can still be found in the eastern savannah.

The Gulf is known for the antiquity of its Aboriginal culture (it is estimated that Aborigines have lived in the region continuously for the last 35,000 years) and the extraordinary richness of its wildlife, including white herons, saltwater crocodiles, possums, wallabies, gliders, the jabiru, pelicans, brolgas, black swans, dugongs and emus.

South of this region, in the heart of outback Queensland, are places which mean a lot to Australians. Combo Waterhole, an undistinguished hole near Kynuna, is said to be the billabong into which Banjo Paterson's 'jolly swagman' jumped. The town of McKinlay was renamed 'Walkabout Creek' for Paul Hogan's *Crocodile Dundee*.

It is true outback – isolated, lonely, and with vast distances separating the main settlements.

DON'T MISS

*** Normanton–Croydon railway journey: one of the great train journeys.
*** Stockman's Hall of Fame, Longreach: excellent introduction to the history of the outback
*** Mt Isa Mines: tour of the underground operations
** John Flynn Museum: located in Cloncurry; history of the Australian Flying Doctor Service.

Opposite: *Flat cattle country characterizes the Gulf region of western Queensland. Windmills bring hot artesian water to the surface in this dry, inhospitable country.*

BURKETOWN

Burketown is a small town on the flat plains of the Gulf near the Albert River. It is a service centre for the surrounding district with a pub, a couple of petrol stations, a council office, and three general stores.

The first Europeans into the area were Burke and Wills who reached the coast near Normanton in 1861. Both Frederick Walker and William Landsborough explored the area while looking for Burke and Wills.

The town originally was a port for the beef industry which spread around it. Today it is still possible to see the **Edkins Brothers Boiling Works** with its boilers, vats, cauldrons and equipment, all shipped originally from Sydney. Beef from the area was successfully salted and smoked for export. By March 1867 the Edkin brothers were exporting cured beef and barrels of tallow to Batavia and Singapore and sending horns, hooves and hides to Brisbane and Sydney for secondary processing.

Artesian Bore **

The hot water from the town's **Artesian Bore** has been rising from the basin for over a century and the minerals in the water have built up so that now it looks more like a piece of modern sculpture than a tap to the hot water underground. The pond around the bore has also been coloured by minerals.

Gulf Country

NORMANTON

This delightful town started life as a port for the cattle industry at the Gulf of Carpentaria. The site of was chosen in 1867 by William Landsborough who had sailed up the Norman River. Over the next decade it became an important port – as indicated by the **Burns Philip** on main street.

Left: *Normanton is a true outback Gulf town. The most distinctive building is the National Hotel in the main street which has been painted a lurid purple. The locals call it 'The Purple Pub'.*

Below: *Brolgas make their way across the dry plains looking for food, and estuarine crocodiles live in the rivers of the Gulf.*

Interesting buildings include the distinctive **'Purple Pub'**, the **'Albion Hotel'** where Captain Percy Tresize drew a series of humorous paintings on the bar room walls. The **Bank of New South Wales**, now a listed National Trust Building, is an unusual building which looks more like a house than a bank.

The town experienced a major boom with the discovery of gold at Croydon in 1885. By 1891 the population had reached 1251. But the gold diggings were short-lived and although the Normanton –Croydon railway line was opened by 1907 the whole area was on the decline.

The Gulflander ★★★
The town's **'The Gulflander'** is the railway line originally planned to service the beef industry by running from Normanton to Cloncurry. Today it carries tourists between Normanton and Croydon.

The **Normanton Railway station** is listed by the National Trust and is an unusual building made distinctive by the decorative patterns on the cross-braces which hold up the corrugated iron roof.

Below: *The large outback township of Mt Isa is dominated, both visually and economically, by its mine which yields vast quantities of silver, lead and zinc.*

KARUMBA

Karumba, the sole port on the Gulf of Carpentaria, is home to both a prawning fleet and Queensland's lucrative barramundi industry. Nestled at the mouth of the Norman River it takes its name from the local Aboriginal tribe.

The old Empire Flying Boats used to stop-over in Karumba to refuel en route to Britain and the flying boat slipway still stands. It was also a military outpost during the second world war.

MOUNT ISA

Mount Isa is the largest city in the world, encompassing 40,977km^2 (15,182 sq miles), and the road from Mount Isa to Camooweal, a distance of 189km (117 miles), is the longest city road in the world.

Mount Isa Mines **

Mount Isa Mines is one of the most highly mechanised and cost efficient mines in the world. It's the world's biggest single producer of silver and lead and is amongst the world's top ten for copper and zinc. As Australia's largest underground mine, it has a daily output of around 35,000 tonnes of ore. A comprehensive tour of the mines is the highlight of any visit to Mount Isa. It is necessary to book well in advance.

Other worthwhile visits include the **Royal Flying Doctor Service** and the **School of the Air**. Both provide vital services for property owners far from the towns.

The views from the **City Lookout** across the city to the mine offer an ideal orientation. At night time the lookout is a popular vantage point as the city's streetlights and the lights of the mines are unusually attractive.

Left: *The John Flynn Museum at Cloncurry is a celebration of the life of the Presbyterian clergyman who brought religion and medicine to the outback. His greatest legacy is the Royal Flying Doctor Service – a recreation of the office is part of the museum.*

CLONCURRY

Copper was discovered in western Queensland at Cloncurry. There the first regular QANTAS flight landed and the first Flying Doctor base was established.

Cloncurry's greatest attraction is the museum dedicated to **Rev. John Flynn (Flynn of the Inland).** John Flynn Place is an excellent overview of the Flynn legacy. It moves progressively from an image of outback conditions at the turn of the century to the history of Flynn himself. The display includes some interesting personal memorabilia and explanations of how the whole Flying Doctor system worked in the early days.

MCKINLAY

McKinlay's great claim to fame is that the local pub, now known as the **Walkabout Creek Hotel**, featured in the original *Crocodile Dundee* as the location where Dundee regularly drank. The town grew as a service centre for the surrounding pastoralists and has remained small, despite the interest generated by *Crocodile Dundee*, with a couple of stores, a few houses and the pub.

JULIA CREEK

In 1928, the first radio call to the newly established flying doctor services was sent from Julia Creek. On an improvised runway the plane was able to land to assist an injured stockman.

CROCODILE DUNDEE COUNTRY

Crocodile Dundee is the most financially successful movie ever made in Australia. The early scenes in the movie depict an outback pub in the middle of nowhere known as the **Walkabout Creek Hotel**. Known originally as the Federal McKinlay Hotel, it is located in the tiny outback settlement of McKinlay. It was sold for $290,000 after the movie had been made and the current owners, while maintaining the rough and tumble feel of the original, are committed to developing it as a tourist attraction.

Today, this isolated township on the Flinders Highway is a very busy livestock trucking and saleyard centre. It is also a major potential supplier of shale oil deposits. Until an economic method of extraction becomes available it will remain a largely undeveloped resource.

The water from the artesian bore in Julia Creek is so hot that most of the houses are equipped with special cooling systems.

Above: *The Corfield & Fitzmaurice general store in the main street of Winton is only a few doors from the North Gregory Hotel where 'Waltzing Matilda' was first performed in public.*

AUSTRALIA'S MOST FAMOUS SONG

Australia's famous 'Waltzing Matilda', was written by the poet 'Banjo' Paterson on Dagworth Station outside the outback town of Winton. No-one knows exactly what prompted Paterson to write his tale of the swaggie who, rather than surrender to the police, decided to commit suicide by jumping into a billabong. But the poem was written on Dagworth Station and when one of the station visitors Christina Macpherson played the tune 'Craiglea' for the guests, Paterson put his lyrics to the music.

WINTON

Most Australians associate Winton with the bush balladeer **Banjo Paterson** and particularly with the writing, and first performance of, **'Waltzing Matilda'**. No-one knows what prompted him to write his tale of the swaggie who jumped into a billabong, but its first public performance was at the **North Gregory Hotel** in Winton. The current hotel is the fourth North Gregory (the other three either burned down or were destroyed) but it is still on the site of the original pub. Paterson's 'jolly' swagman has been immortalised, albeit in fibreglass, and appropriately he sits near a very healthy looking coolabah tree.

Nearby is the **Qantilda Museum**, a collection of memorabilia of the area including displays of old machinery, a recreation of Christina Macpherson playing 'Craiglea' and an extensive display of QANTAS material.

Lark Quarry Environmental Park ★★★

The park, south of Winton, with its famous **Dinosaur Stampede**, is an interesting insight into life in western Queensland some 95 million years ago. This is the largest group of footprints of running dinosaurs uncovered anywhere in the world. First discovered in the early 1960s it was completely excavated in 1976–77. Three species of dinosaur made the 1200 tracks – a large flesh eating carnosaur and many small coelurosaurs and ornithopods.

Longreach ★★★

Longreach has grown from a camp for teamsters carrying supplies to the region's vast properties to the largest town in central Queensland. Situated on the Thomson River it is the centre of a prosperous wool and beef area. The two major attractions are its association with the establishment of QANTAS and its excellent Stockman's Hall of Fame.

QANTAS, known at the time as the Queensland and Northern Territory Aerial Services Ltd., was set up on 16 November 1920 by Hudson Fysh and Paul McGinness. Local graziers funded the airline and in 1921 a hangar was built. It became an important maintenance depot and in 1926 it was converted to a workshop where seven DH50 biplanes were constructed. The hangar, which is nothing but a large shed, is located at the airport opposite the Stockman's Hall of Fame south of the town.

> **STOCKMAN'S HALL OF FAME**
>
> The A$12.5 million **Australian Stockman's Hall of Fame and Outback Heritage Centre** should more accurately be called 'The Australian History Timeline'. Opened in 1988 by Queen Elizabeth II, it is an excellent way to become acquainted with the life and history of Australia. The artist Hugh Sawrey first touted the idea of a museum to tribute early outback pioneers, and with support from the government it grew to encompass a comprehensive look at all aspects of Australian history.

Australian Stockman's Hall of Fame and Outback Heritage Centre ★★★

The $12.5 million centre has made Longreach the premier destination in central Queensland. It should more accurately be called 'The Australian History Timeline'. Its exhibitions include a model of Aboriginal cave paintings, the first fleet (with a computerised list of all the people on the First Fleet), the early settlement in Sydney, the major explorations, the early pioneers (with a model slab hut, a hawker's van and a blacksmith's shop) the pastoral expansion, and then a focus on life in the bush up to the present day. It is easy to spend about four or five hours just exploring the fascinating displays on the time line.

Below: *Standing like an oasis in the flat lands of western Queensland, the Stockman's Hall of Fame is a tourist attraction which celebrates the conquest of outback Australia.*

The Gulf Country at a Glance

The Gulf Country becomes hot and humid as the wet season settles in during the summer months of December through to February. The roads are subject to flooding and the many dirt roads in the area become quite impassable at this time. The best time to visit is **March** to **November** when the days are sunny and the weather, although often quite hot, is usually dry and pleasant.

GETTING THERE

The distances are vast and the roads are often little more than satisfactory. People wanting to explore the area should hire or purchase a 4WD vehicle. If you want to restrict yourself to the main centres all the roads are sealed and a conventional sedan will suffice.

Both **Greyhound/ Pioneer**, tel: 13 2030 and **McCafferty's**, tel: 13 1499 run coach services in the area. **Rail** services to Mt Isa and Cloncurry is via Townsville and run twice a week, Wednesday and Sunday. Brisbane to Longreach runs Tuesday and Friday. For further information ring, tel: 13 2232.

Ansett, tel: 131 300 have regular flights to Mt Isa, Cloncurry, Longreach and Winton.

The area is crossed by two major highways. The Flinders Highway runs from Townsville to Mt. Isa and the Matilda Highway from Cloncurry to Winton and Longreach. The distances are great but the **roads** are flat.

GETTING AROUND

Cloncurry and Mt Isa are relatively large centres in this remote area and offer taxi services within the towns. Check with the Tourist Information centres listed in useful contacts. **Hertz RentaCar**, tel: (07) 4743-4142 operates out of Mt Isa and offers a wide selection of cars and 4WD vehicles. Longreach and Winton have taxi services. Check with the local tourist information centre. There is a coach tour service in Longreach (see **Tours and Excursions** on p. 111).

WHERE TO STAY

Cloncurry

Cloncurry is a medium-sized service centre for the surrounding rural area. Accommodation is limited.

BUDGET

Cloncurry Wagon Wheel Motel, 54 Ramsay Street, tel: (07) 4742-1866. Licensed restaurant and comfortable rooms with swimming pool. **Oasis Motel**, Ramsay Street, tel: (07) 4742-1366. Air-conditioning in all rooms with a comfortable standard of accommodation.

Mt Isa

A major mining centre which has a wide range of accommodation from 4-star motels to budget accommodation. **Burke and Wills Isa Resort**, cnr Camooweal and Grace Streets. tel: (07) 4743-8000. Quality motel, licensed restaurant and excellent facilities. **Copper City Motel**, 105 Butler Street, tel: (07) 4743-3233. Comfortable standard with pool and air conditioning in all rooms.

BUDGET

Silver Star Motel, Marian Street, tel: (07) 4743-3466. Comfortable accommodation at a budget price.

Winton

The birth place of QANTAS airlines, site for the composition of 'Waltzing Matilda', and an interesting stop over between Longreach and Mt Isa. Accommodation is limited to a number of motels and rural hotels. **Matilda Motel**, 20 Oondooroo Street, tel: (07) 4657-1433. Comfortable airconditioned rooms, dinner to units. **The Outback Motel**, 95 Elderslie Street, tel: (07) 4657-1422. Offers a good standard of room with airconditioning.

Longreach

Longreach has become a major tourist destination in this area and offers a reasonable range of accommodation.

The Gulf Country at a Glance

Albert Park Motel,
Sir Hudson Fysh Dr,
tel: (07) 4658-2411,
fax: 4658-3181.
Close to the Stockman's
Hall of Fame – licensed
restaurant, pool and spa.

Longreach Motor Inn,
84 Galah Street, tel: (07)
4658-2322, fax: 4658-1828.
57 units with airconditioning
and a licensed restaurant.

Jumbuck Motel, Sir Hudson
Fysh Dr, tel: (07) 4658-1799,
fax: 4658-1832. Licensed
restaurant and some rooms
with inter-connecting doors
makes this an excellent
family motel.

BUDGET
Starlight Motel, Wonga
Street, (07) 4658-1288, fax:
4658-3277. A small motel
with a good standard
of accommodation.

WHERE TO EAT

Cloncurry
Cloncurry has road houses
and cafés. The better quality
licensed restaurants are
located in the town's motels.
**Cloncurry Wagon Wheel
Motel**, 54 Ramsay Street,
tel: (07) 4742-1866.
Licensed restaurant.

Mt Isa
The wide selection of
restaurants in Mt Isa
reflects the larger popu-
lation. Motels and hotels
still provide the best eating
facilities in town.

**Explorers Restaurant at
Burke and Wills Isa Resort**,
cnr Camooweal and Grace
streets. tel: (07) 4743-8000.
Licensed restaurant that prides
itself on its barramundi –
a superb local fish.

Abyssinia Café Restaurant,
103 Marian Street, tel: (07)
4743-9399. Indoor or outdoor
dining in the heart of Mt Isa.

Winton
There are a few roadhouses
and cafés in Winton. The
local hotels offer meals.

Longreach
**Happy Valley Chinese
Restaurant**, 135 Eagle
Street, tel: (07) 4658-1311.
Family restaurant that
is fully licensed.

Albert Park Motel,
Sir Hudson Fysh Drive,
tel: (07) 4658-2411.
Licensed restaurant.

**Bush Verandah
Restaurant**, 120 Galah
Street, tel: (07) 4658-2322.
Home-style restaurant.

Longreach Motor Inn,
84 Galah Street, tel: (07)
4658-2322. Licensed restaurant attached to the motel
open to general public.

TOURS AND EXCURSIONS

**Campbell's Coaches
Copper City Tours**, Mt Isa,
tel: (07) 4743-2006. Offers
a fullday tour of the mine
or a threeday safari visiting
fossil sites and Lawn Hill
Gorge National Park.

Mount Isa Mines Tours,
Visitors Centre, tel: (07)
4744-2011. Conducted sur-
face and underground tour
of this famous mine.

Outback Aussie Tours,
Longreach, toll free
1300 787 890. Offering
a variety of tours in this
fascinating area.

**Longreach Outback Travel
Tours**, 115A Eagle Street,
tel: (07) 4658-1776. A tour
company that will arrange
the tour of your choice
plus accommodation.

Billabong Boat Cruises,
115A Eagle Street,
tel: (07) 4658-1776.
Cruising the beautiful
Thomson River, Star and
Dinner Cruise a favourite.

USEFUL CONTACTS

**John Flynn Place
Museum**, cnr King and
Daintree Streets, tel: (07)
4727-4100.

**Mount Isa, Riversleigh
Fossil Display and
Information Centre**,
19 Marian Street, tel: (07)
4749-1555.

**Winton Information
Centre located in
Gift and Gem Centre**,
Elderslie Street,
tel: (07) 4657-1296.

**Longreach Tourist
Information Centre**,
Qantas Park,
tel: (07) 4658-3555 or
Shire Council Office,
Eagle Street,
tel: (07) 4658-4111.

9
Darling Downs and Far West

South of the Gulf Country, inland from Brisbane, heading west beyond the Great Dividing Range, the vast grassy flat area of the **Darling Downs** slowly gives way to savanna grassland and finally desert. The towns are isolated, the distances between them long, and the roads are sealed only to the width of a single car. The accommodation is rustic and often the only water supply bubbles up from hundreds of metres below the surface through artesian bores. Most of the area is flat and seems to roll on forever. The people of this region regard their lonely existence with considerable pride and hardiness.

By the 1860s graziers had moved through **Cunningham's Gap** to reach the Darling Downs and established huge sheep and cattle stations on the vast grassy slopes. Allan Cunningham, who discovered the gap in the mountain range, always regarded his discovery of the rich and fertile Darling Downs, and the prospect of easy access from the coast as his major achievement.

Further west the area becomes marginal agricultural land with small rainfall supported by the subterranean artesian basin. Some 100km (62 miles) to the west of **Birdsville** it ceases to be even marginal when the edge of the **Simpson Desert National Park** is reached.

Although the area has been given over to sheep and cattle it is noted for the rich diversity of its native wildlife. Brolgas, flocks of black and white cockatoos, wild pigs, corellas (which are native to the area), kangaroos and emus abound.

DON'T MISS

*** Stanthorpe's wineries: lie to the south of the town.
*** Eulo and Yowah: strange outback towns dependent on opal mining
** Birdsville: one of Australia's most isolated and famous outback towns
** Warwick: impressive and gracious town with lots of historic buildings.

Opposite: *Beyond the Darling Downs and the Matilda Highway, western Queensland becomes an inhospitable desert of red sand dunes and scrubby desert bushes.*

Two rivers, the dusty Diamantina and Cooper Creek, run through the area. If the rains of the monsoonal wet season reach the headwaters of these rivers large areas of the southwest can be converted into a vast lake. In periods of drought the waterways become little more than a series of muddy holes.

Above: *Warwick has many impressive buildings in Palmerin Street including Johnson's buildings (with their elaborate façade) which date from 1913.*
Opposite: *When Queensland became an independent state it established customs houses along its border with NSW. The old Customs House at Goondiwindi is now a museum.*

This is still frontier land. It is harsh and inhospitable with roads only suitable for 4WD vehicles. The mythology of outback Australia looms large and stockmen still enjoy a near-legendary status.

WARWICK

Warwick is an attractive town just past Cunningham's Gap. It can claim to be the first important settlement in inland Queensland.

Palmerin Street has many beautiful historic buildings. The **Post Office** (1891) is a huge two-storey building with Saracenic arches on the first floor, a large cupola and Tuscan columns on the ground floor. It was built from locally quarried sandstone. The **Town Hall** (1888) was also constructed from local sandstone and is distinguished by a large, elegant clock tower. **St Marys Church** (1864) is a sandstone Gothic Revival building distinguished by its lancet windows and large rose window on the eastern side, and the **Criterion Hotel** (1917) retains much of its early charm.

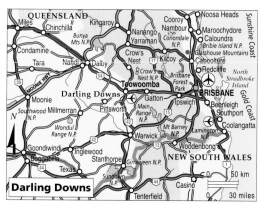

Darling Downs

In recent times Warwick has promoted itself as the **'Rose and Rodeo City'** because of the fame of the Warwick Rodeo which is held each October. Warwick is the headquarters of the Australian Rough Riders Association and it proudly boasts that George Leslie held the first rodeo on Canning Downs back in the 1860s.

STANTHORPE

Further west is Stanthorpe, a remarkably pretty town in the middle of a rich, mixed-farming area of vineyards, orchards and sheep and cattle grazing.

Stanthorpe is unusually cool for Queensland. In winter night temperatures often fall below zero – the average minimum temperature for July is 0.3°C (32°F). The temperature in the town once fell to –14.6°C (25°F), the coldest ever recorded in Queensland.

To the south are many interesting wineries including **Elsinore Wines** in the tiny settlement of **Glen Aplin**, **Kominos Wines** near Severnlea, **Granite Belt Vignerons**, **Stone Ridge Vineyards and Winery**, **Bungawarra Wines** at Ballendean and **Winewood Wineries**.

GOONDIWINDI

On the border and located 362km (225 miles) from Brisbane, Goondiwindi is a typical rambling Queensland settlement spreading out from the old **Customs House** on the banks of the Macintyre River.

In the 1840s it was a riverside camp for the teamsters bringing supplies from northern New South Wales to the outlying properties in western Queensland. This importance was greatly increased when Queensland became a separate colony in 1859. The establishment of the Customs House ensured the settlement's continuing importance.

CLIMATE

The climate in the Darling Downs and Far West varies hugely. Places like Stanthorpe and Texas have been known to experience snow in the winter months while Birdsville suffers from the extremes of continentality with very hot days (over 40°C/104°F in summertime) and nights below freezing in the winter. The rains decline towards the west with Birdsville receiving less than 150mm (6 in) per year while the rainfall on the Darling Downs is typically around 750mm (29½ in).

The **Customs House** was probably first built in 1859 but over the years it has gone through a number of alterations. Between 1872–1894 it operated as a centre for a staff employed to police and control illegal trading between Queensland and New South Wales.

Today the town is in the heart of a large cotton growing area. The **Macintyre Cotton Gin** actually encourages visits. It is open daily from 08:00–17:00 between April and September.

Above: *The area around Goondiwindi has become a major cotton producer. In season the paddocks and the roads are covered with cotton balls.*

BEYOND GOONDIWINDI
Eulo **

Eulo's charm makes it more than just another outback town with a pub and general store. As you enter the town, on the right before the Eulo Queen pub, is the famous 'Paroo Track' where the world lizard-racing championships are held. Called the **Cunnamulla-Eulo Festival of Opals** it occurs in late August/early September. The Herbie Trophy is awarded for the fastest time. The world record of 1.2 seconds was set in 1983 by a lizard, 'Spikey'.

THE EULO LIZARD RACE

Eulo is famous for the town's **'Paroo Track'** where **world lizard racing championships** are held each August. At the left hand side of the track is a piece of granite with a plaque which reads: 'Cunnamulla-Eulo Festival of Opals. "Destructo" champion racing cockroach accidentally killed at this track (24.8.1980) after winning the challenge (sic) stakes against "Wooden Head" champion racing lizard 1980. Unveiled 23.8.81'. Somehow the spelling mistake, the absurdity of a cockroach racing a lizard, the imagined circumstances under which the cockroach got accidentally trodden on, all make for something which gives the town an immediate charm.

Out of Eulo on the road to Thargomindah is a sign which reads: '**Mud Springs**'. Built up over centuries these springs and others like them were the original release valves for the Great Artesian Basin. The tops are soft and jelly like and are the release valves. Occasionally they do explode with a loud report audible for miles.'

Yowah **

Yowah has been an opal field for nearly a century. In the 1890s its population grew to 400–500 but today it ranges from about 50 in summer to about 100 in winter as people, mostly Victorians, seek the Queensland warmth in winter. This is surprising as this lonely place has no electricity, relies on bore water, and the Flying Doctor is still the only reliable medical service. However, there are the valuable opal deposits known as 'Yowah Nuts'. To the uninitiated they look like rocks but when split open they sometimes contain a centre of pure opal.

Opposite below:
The most prominent building in Eulo is the Eulo Queen Hotel in the main street. It was named after Isabel MacIntosh who became known as the Opal Queen of Eulo.

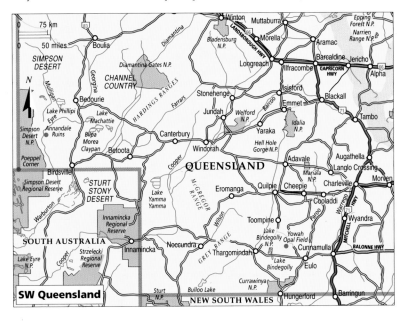

Thargomindah

Thargomindah is the last hint of civilisation before the traveller heads off towards the remote area of Cameron Corner where the borders of Queensland, New South Wales and South Australia meet.

The town's **artesian bore** was drilled in 1891, and by 1893 reached a depth of 795m (2607ft) before water came to the surface. The pressure of the bore water, uniquely, was used to drive a generator to supply electricity until 1951. Today the bore is still the main water supply with a surface temperature of 84°C (183°F).

Charleville ✶✶

Charleville, on the way to Birdsville, is an attractive town on the banks of the Warrego River. The town's **'Historical House'** in Alfred Street was built in 1881 as the local branch of the Queensland National Bank with the teller's area, the safe and the manager's office at the front and accommodation for the manager's family, including the maid's quarters, at the back. The historical society have preserved the original functions and filled each room with appropriate pieces of furniture and memorabilia.

Charleville's **Royal Flying Doctor Service** serves the whole of southern Queensland, and it is open for inspection from 08:00–16:00 daily. The base in Charleville is very proud of the fact that visitors are taken through a working operation. There is no charge but donations are appreciated.

Birdsville ✶✶

Birdsville is 1600km (994 miles) west of Brisbane and, like some kind of mysterious magnet, attracts people to this most isolated place on the continent. Originally named Diamantina Crossing, it was renamed Birdsville by the owner of Pandie Pandie Station who was amazed by the diversity of bird life which inhabited the area. It is extraordinary to find seagulls in the salt lakes which exist in the area.

Birdsville was established as a custom collecting point in the 1880s when Queensland could still levy a toll on stock coming through from South Australia. Drovers and station owners in western Queensland realised that moving cattle through the Channel country and down the Birdsville Track to the railhead at Marree (which had been opened in 1884) was the most efficient way to get cattle to the coastal markets. Pre-federation Queensland established a customs collection point at Birdsville which was only 10km (6 miles) from the border. By the late 1880s the town boasted two hotels, three general stores, a doctor, a bank and a police magistrate.

The old **Australian Inland Mission Hospital** is a wonderful rough stone building constructed in 1882 as the Royal Hotel, one of the town's two pubs. It was bought by the AIM in 1923 and used as a hospital base for the Royal Flying Doctor. It was from this building that Birdsville's first pedal wireless broadcast occurred in 1929.

The second pub, the **Birdsville Hotel**, was built in 1884–5. A simple, stone, single storey, building it is now listed by the National Trust. It has become something of a mandatory stopover point in the town. During September when the town's spring races are held and people fly and drive in from all over Australia, the pub does a roaring trade.

Poeppel Corner *

In the dry Simpson Desert the border of Queensland, Northern Territory and South Australia converge at Poeppel Corner. Augustus Poeppel placed a surveyor's peg here in 1880. The peg was found in 1962 and today a monument, accessible only via a 150km (93 mile) track from Birdsville, marks this furthermost point of far west Queensland.

Above: *One of the most famous of all outback events is the Birdsville Races. Held in spring they attract people from all over Australia, most of whom fly into the town's tiny airport.*

Opposite: *Given that Birdsville has only one small pub, the Birdsville races stretch the town's very limited resources to the limit.*

BIRDSVILLE RACES

The Birdsville Hotel was built in 1884–5. This simple, stone, single-storey building is now listed by the National Trust. It has become something of a mandatory stopover point in the town. During September when the town's spring races are held and people fly and drive in from all over Australia the pub does a roaring trade. The races are usually held in early September. They raise money for the Royal Flying Doctor Service.

Darling Downs and Far West at a Glance

The summer time temperatures in this area can reach as high as 50°C (122°F). So the best time to travel in the far west is during the winter months when the days are warm and sunny and the nights are cold. However, closer to the coast around Warwick and Stanthorpe the winters can be extremely cold and the best seasons to visit are the spring and autumn. Often the summer months can be quite pleasant on the Darling Downs although they can be very hot and dry.

The Darling Downs covers a large area from Toowoomba across to Goondiwindi. Beyond Goondiwindi the land becomes increasing drier and the distances become greater. From Goondiwindi to Birdsville the distances are great and the roads are lonely so care should be taken. If travelling by **car** Warwick is 115km (71 miles) west from Brisbane on the Cunningham Highway (Highway 15). Stanthorpe is 61km (38 miles) south from Warwick on the New England Highway and to get to Goondiwindi continue west on the Cunningham Highway for another 201km (125 miles). From Goondiwindi travel to St George and head west to Cunnamulla, then north on

the Matilda Highway to Charleville and further west is Birdsville. The journey from Goondiwindi to Birdsville is 1796km (1115 miles). The **coach** company **Greyhound/Pioneer**, tel: 13 2030, travel to Warwick, Stanthorpe and Goondiwindi, check for timetable. **McCafferty's**, tel: 13 1499, offer a service to all of these towns plus a package to Birdsville during the Birdsville races (September). For **rail** information and timetables tel: 132 232. **Ansett** fly to Birdsville. Check for timetable 131 300.

Warwick and Stanthorpe have car hire and taxi facilities and a local bus service. *See also* the information centres listed under **Useful Contacts** on p. 121. Goondiwindi has car hire facilities check with Tourist Information.

This is outback Queensland. Consequently the towns are serviced by modest motels and pubs. Do not expect to find 4-star accommodation.

Warwick
Located on the Condamine River a rural city with many historic buildings built of local sandstone.
McNevins Gunyah Motel, cnr New England Highway and Glen Rd, tel: (07) 4611-

5588, fax: 4661-5588. Small motel but with all the facilities of a larger motel, licensed restaurant and pool. **Village Motor Inn**, 57 Victoria Street, tel: (07) 4661-1699. Good standard of accommodation, centrally located. **Alexander Motel**, cnr Wood and Wentworth streets, tel: (07) 4661-3888, fax: 4661-5889. Quiet setting and panoramic views over Warwick mountains.

Stanthorpe
Wine growing area offering the traveller a beautiful town to explore with the added bonus of several National Parks.
Happy Valley Homestead Resort, Glenlyon Drive, tel: (07) 4681-3250, fax: 4681-3082. This resort offers different standards of accommodation. Open fires and real country cooking, wine tours offered.
Apple and Grape Motel, 63 Maryland Street, tel: (07) 4681-1288. Family motel offering playground and recreation room.
Stannum Lodge Motor Inn, 12 Wallangarra Rd, tel: (07) 4681-2000, fax: 4681-1045. Pool BBQ area and good location
Boulevard Hotel, 76 Maryland Street, tel: (07) 4681-1777, fax: 4681-3218. Central location and good standard rooms offering tea making facilities.

Darling Downs and Far West at a Glance

Goondiwindi

Located on the banks of the MacIntyre River – the Queensland–New South Wales Border.

The Town House Motor Inn, 110 Marshall Street, tel: (07) 4671-1855, or toll free 1800 076 666. Award-winning motel offering a high standard of accommodation and excellent licensed restaurant.

Pioneer Motor Inn, 145 Marshall Street, tel: (07) 4671-2888. Luxury units, pool and laundry facilities.

Binalong Motel, 30 McLean Street, tel: (07) 4671-1777. Small well-priced motel with all the amenities.

Birdsville

The Hotel and the Birdsville Races held every September are the major attractions for this tiny outback settlement.

Birdsville Hotel, Main Street, tel: (07) 4656-3244, fax: 4656-3262. Historic hotel that offers a comfortable standard of accommodation.

WHERE TO EAT

Warwick

McNevins Gunyah Motel, cnr New England Highway and Glen Rd, tel: (07) 4661-5588. This motel offers a fully licensed restaurant with friendly service.

Elms Family Restaurant, Albion Street, tel: (07) 4661-2449. Good service and wholesome cooking make this a favourite restaurant.

Roses Restaurant, Wood Street. tel: (07) 4661-3777. Small restaurant with home cooking and relaxed atmosphere.

Stanthorpe

Boulevard Court Chinese Restaurant, 68 Maryland Street, tel: (07) 4681-2828. Chinese cooking for the whole family.

Anna's Restaurant, cnr Wallangarra Rd and O'Mara, (07) 4681-1265.

Happy Valley Homestead Restaurant, Amiens Rd via Stanthorpe, tel: (07) 4681-3250. Worth the short trip – country cooking at it best in a rural environment.

Goondiwindi

The Town House Motor Inn, 110 Marshall Street, tel: (07) 4671-1855, or toll free 1800 076 666. Award-winning licensed restaurant, cuisine that will please all tastes.

Rustlers Steakhouse Restaurant, 151 Marshall Street, tel: (07) 4671-2555. Licensed restaurant with rustic period atmosphere offers inside and outside dining.

Victoria Hotel, Marshall Street, tel: (07) 4671-1007. This grand old hotel offers a licensed restaurant that offers a good wholesome meal.

Birdsville

Birdsville Hotel, Main Street, tel: (07) 4656-3244. Historic hotel with restaurant.

TOURS AND EXCURSIONS

McCafferty's Coaches, tel: 13 1499 offer comprehensive tours throughout this region. They are a family owned company and are extremely helpful.

Goondiwindi Travel Centre, 39 Marshall Street, tel: (07) 4671-1677. The staff will be happy to help with organising tours or advising you on the tours that will suit your needs.

USEFUL CONTACTS

The information centres in all of the towns are informative and the staff are happy to help with advice and tours. They will also recommend and book accommodation.

Southern Downs Tourist Association, Albion Street, tel: (07) 4661-3122.

Southern Downs Tourist Association, 28 Leslie Parade, tel: (07) 4681-2057.

Goondiwindi Tourist Information Centre, McLean Street (under the water tower), tel: (07) 4671-2653, The centre is well equipped to provide travellers with a wide range of useful information about Birdsville.

• Before heading into the beautiful National Parks that are in the area please check with the local National Parks and Wildlife Service. **Warwick Parks and Wildlife**, contact Toowoomba Office, tel: (07) 4639-4599.

Travel Tips

Tourist Information

The Australian Tourist Commission provides good material free of charge and is located in major international cities, as well as Australian capital cities. There are excellent information centres in Brisbane.All areas throughout Queensland have tourist information centres clearly marked, supplying maps, brochures and information on accommodation, transport, restaurants and tours. Open 09:00–17:30 on weekdays and Saturday mornings:

The Queensland Government Travel Centre, cnr Adelaide and Edward streets, Brisbane 4000, tel: (07) 3221-6111, fax: 3221-5320.

Queensland National Parks & Wildlife Service, Ann Street, Brisbane 4000, tel: (07) 3227-7111, fax: 3227-6534.

Brisbane Area

Greater Brisbane Tourist Association, Transit Centre, Roma Street, tel: (07) 3236-3355, fax: 3236-1126.

Toowoomba Tourist Information Centre, 541 Ruthven Street,Toowoomba, tel: (07) 4639-3797, fax: 4632-4044.

Ipswich Regional Tourist Information Centre, Cnr D'Arcy Doyle Place and Brisbane Street, Ipswich, tel: (07) 3281-0555, fax: 3281-0555.

Gold Coast

Gold Coast Tourism Bureau, Head Office, Level 2, 64 Ferny Ave, Surfers Paradise, tel: (07) 5592-2699, fax: 5570-3144.

Gold Coast Information Centre, cnr Griffith and Warner Streets, Coolangatta, tel: (07) 5536-7765, fax: 5536-7841. Cavill Mall, Surfers Paradise, tel: (07) 5538-4419, fax: 5570-3259.

Sunshine Coast

Noosa Junction Tourist Information, 5/20 Sunshine beach Road, Noosa Heads, tel: (07) 5447-3798.

Gympie Tourist Information Centre, Bruce Hwy, Gympie, tel: (07) 5483-5554, fax: 5482-8205.

Central Coast

Hervey Bay Information Centre, 333 The Esplanade, Scarness, tel: (07) 4124-6911.

Bundaberg Tourist Information Centre, Bourbong Street, Bundaberg, tel: (07) 4152-2333, fax: 4153-1444.

Rockhampton Tourist Information Centre, Quay Street, tel: (07) 4922-5339.

Townsville Information Centre, Flinders Mall, tel: (07) 4721-3660.

Far North

Cairns Tourist Information Centre, Cnr Esplanade and Shields Sts, tel: (07) 4031-1751.

Cooktown Tourist Information Centre, Biard Road, tel: (07) 4069-5755.

Far West

Mount Isa, Riversleigh Fossil Display and Information Centre, 19 Marian St, tel: (07) 4749-1555, fax: 4743-6296.

Longreach Tourist Information Centre, Qantas Park, Longreach, tel: (07) 4658-3555, fax: 4658-3733.

Southern Downs Tourist Association, Albion Street, Warwick, tel: (07) 4661-3122, fax: 4661-1957.

Southern Downs Tourist Association, 28 Leslie Pde, tel/fax: (07) 4681-2057.

Goondiwindi Tourist Information Centre, McLean

Street, Goondiwindi, tel: (07) 4671-2653, fax: 4671-3013.

Visitor centres and offices of the National Parks and Wildlife Service provide material for areas under their jurisdiction and the National Trust offer free walking tour guides from their offices or from tourist centres. A useful source is the RACQ which provides free maps for members of affiliated organisations abroad Their address is: Royal Automobile Club of Queensland, GPO Building, Quant, Brisbane, tel: (070) 3361-2565, fax: 3220-0029.

Entry Requirements

There are no special requirements to enter Queensland from anywhere in Australia. To enter Australia a valid passport is required and, unless you are a New Zealander, you will need a visa. This can be obtained from an Australian consular office or, if you are an American travelling by QANTAS, from the airline's offices in Los Angeles or San Francisco.
Short-stay visas (free) are valid for up to 3 months. Extensions from within Australia can be costly. Furthermore, the amount of time you plan to spend in the country is not entirely at your own discretion. Officials might limit your time if you appear 'unsavoury' in their eyes. A return ticket and 'sufficient funds' are also required, although the meaning of the latter is clearly debatable.
A Working Holiday Maker visa exists for 'young' people (usually meaning 18 to 30) from Japan, Netherlands, Canada,

the UK, Ireland, Republic of Korea, Germany and Malta. The visa is available from the country of origin and costs A$150 charge. It permits casual employment only. most countries now offer short term travellers visas via Electronic Travel Authority or ETA from travel agents. There are no fees or stamps. The visa is for 3 months and has multiple entry. It permits casual rather than full-time employment. Long stay visas are for 3 months to a year and cost $36. Fruit picking is one of the most common, short-term job prospects.
Visa extensions can take time and a A$50 fee must be paid up-front and is not refundable, regardless of the outcome.

Customs

Australian Customs carry out searches at international airports. They are interested in weapons (even if they are ceremonial), drugs and contraband. Passengers must fill out a Customs Declaration before arriving, which also enquires about the importation of products such as leather, feathers, food and timber, and requires visitors to state whether they have visited a farm prior to travel. Australia has managed to avoid many of the flora and fauna problems common to other countries and customs are eager to prevent the arrival of diseases and pests. Duty Free applies to people over the age of 18. Limits are 250 cigarettes or 250g (8¾ ounces) of cigars or tobacco, 1 litre (1¾ pints) of wine or spirits and gifts valued over A$400. Amounts exceeding these limits will

attract import duty to be paid at the arrival point. Import duty rates vary from item to item.

Health Requirements

There are no vaccination or immunization requirements, but if you come from a country, or have recently visited a country, where there is cholera, smallpox or similar highly contagious diseases check with your local Australian embassy or consulate. Health certificates may be required. Australia has no contagious diseases which need to be vaccinated against.

Getting There

By Air: Book flights well in advance. Brisbane and Cairns airports are the state's major international airports. Most international carriers are based in Sydney and Melbourne, so you may need to pass through customs in Sydney and take a connecting flight to Queensland. In Queensland airport bus services provide transport into the city and there are private bus lines which serve most top hotels. See also **At a Glance** sections. You will need to keep A$25 aside for departure tax.
By Road: There is a very clear division between inland and coastal roads. The built-up coastal area from the NSW border to Gympie and west to Toowoomba is served by modern freeways and good quality roads. The further west, the more substandard the roads become. In the far west the roads can be unsealed and around the Gulf it is common for a road to be only a single width of a car. This means that

if you come across a road train (they can be over 20m/65ft long) carrying cattle you have to head off the road.

What to Pack

Queensland enjoys long hot summers and mild winters, but there are variations. Remember:
• The coast is subject to heavy rains during the summer.
• In summer sunny days have a very high UV factor and may seriously burn the skin.
• Summer along Queensland's coast is characterised by very high humidity.
• Inland Queensland has hot, dry days and nights – temperatures can drop below zero.
• Although a largely tropical state there are areas (particularly around Stanthorpe) where temperatures can be very cold. People dress informally, but 'smart casual' wear is often required after dark at theatres, restaurants and sophisticated hotels. Beach wear is acceptable only on the beach and in pubs and fast-food outlets; casual clothing is customary. For summer (Oct–April) pack lightweight clothes and a hat. The Queensland coast has summer rains, so take an umbrella. In winter, usually a lightweight overcoat and woollen garments are needed. Remember warmer clothes are required if going inland.

Money Matters

Bank hours are usually 09:30–16:30 Mon–Thurs, 09:30–17:00 Fri. In the city centre hours can be 08:00–18:00 Mon–Fri. Building societies are often open longer than banks.

Traveller's cheques are readily dealt with, particularly if made out in Australian dollars, and receive a better exchange rate than foreign currency. Virtually all banks will change both, but charges vary so shop around. Credit cards are widely used (preferred by car rental agencies) but may not be welcome in remote areas or smaller shops. In Australia there are 100 cents to the dollar. Coins come in 5c, 10c, 20c, 50c, $1 and $2 denominations and there are A$5, A$10, A$20, A$50 and A$100 notes. Any amount can be taken in and out of the country, but for over A$5000 you must fill in a report form. You could open a cashcard account with a bank, allowing 24hr access to automatic tellers, which are very widespread. You may withdraw A$400 to A$800 a day and can make calls in special phone booths throughout the country. They are also linked to the 'EFTPOS' system allowing you to pay for goods and services in certain stores.

Accommodation

There is a comprehensive guide to accommodation in Australia, with a section on Brisbane and

Queensland, put out by the NRMA, 151 Clarence Street, Sydney NSW 2000, tel: 13 11 22. It is also available from any of the NRMA and RACQ outlets.

Eating Out

Queensland has a variety of eateries in the large centres along the coast (with anything from good seafood and Thai cuisine to McDonald's and KFC), but more restricted eating facilities in the smaller inland centres. Produce is fresh and prices very reasonable – particularly compared to Europe.

Transport

By Air: There are a wide range of domestic air carriers, including **QANTAS** and **Ansett**. *See* the **At A Glance** sections of this book for specific regions. Dial Telstra enquiries, or consult the directories.

By Road: Brisbane and environs are easily accessible by public transport, but hire a car if you want to explore further. There are a large number of rental agencies and major companies – **Avis**, **Hertz** and **Budget** – operate at most major airports. They differ little on rentals but competition may mean short-

CONVERSION CHART		
FROM	TO	MULTIPLY BY
Millimetres	Inches	0.0394
Metres	Yards	1.0936
Metres	Feet	3.281
Kilometres	Miles	0.6214
Kilometres square	Square miles	0.386
Hectares	Acres	2.471
Litres	Pints	1.760
Kilograms	Pounds	2.205
Tonnes	Tons	0.984
To convert Celsius to Fahrenheit: x 9 ÷ 5 + 32		

term specials. Unlimited kilometre rates are common around cities, but remote driving can incur a higher rate plus a kilometre charge – and there are insurance expenses. Smaller companies may be cheaper, so consult the *Yellow Pages* (Telstra telephone Business Directory). A valid driving licence is essential and applicants must usually be over 21. Information about travelling in Queensland can be obtained from the **Royal Automobile Club of Queensland** (see p.123). Queenslander's drive on the left of the road and the road signs conform with standard international regulations.
By Bus: Two coach companies, **Greyhound/Pioneer**, tel: (07) 3840-9364 or toll free 13 2030, and **McCafferty's**, tel: (07) 2326-3033 (toll free 13 1499) offer services from Brisbane.
Trains: The Transit Centre in Roma Street, Brisbane, is the main terminus and booking point for long-distance trains. For information on **Countrylink Rail Services**, toll free 13 2232.

Business Hours

These are 08:30/09:00–17:00/ 17:30 weekdays, 09:00–13:00 Saturday, with late-night shopping on Thursday and/or Friday, when the shops close at 20:00/ 21:00. But these hours vary in different centres. Some shops close 16:00 Saturday and some open Sundays. Major chains in densely populated areas tend to stay open longer, and milk bars, delis, corner shops, and city bookshops also boast extended trading.

Time Difference

Queensland is 10 hours ahead of Greenwich mean time. ie. when it is Noon at GMT it is 22:00 in Queensland.

Communications

Post Offices are open 09:00– 17:00 Mon–Fri, and provide comprehensive postal and fax services. Public telephones, particularly in rural areas, are located near the GPO. Overseas rates are high. Some Post Offices in suburban areas and shopping malls are open on Saturday. Telephone enquiry services are offered by **Telstra**: dial **12455**

Electricity Supply

The electrical current is 220– 240 volts AC. The local plug-and-socket system uses three pins. These are not the same as those in the UK and only top hotels have appropriate converters. Hardware stores may carry adaptors, but an Australian plug may also be fitted.

Weights and Measures

Australia is metric. Distances are measured in kilometres, petrol and drinks are in litres, temperature in centrigrade, and food is measured in grams and kilograms.

Health Precautions

Australia has high standards of hygiene and very safe food and water, so precautions are unnecessary. But there are three major health problems, in Queensland particularly:
• The skin cancer rate is high so apply sun cream and wear a broad-brimmed hat and a shirt with a collar and long sleeves.

PUBLIC HOLIDAYS

The major holidays in Queensland include:
1 January •
New Year's Day
26 January • Australia Day
Easter • Good Friday and Easter Monday
25 April • Anzac Day
25–26 December •
Christmas Day & Boxing Day

Queenslanders commonly take their holidays during the school summer vacation, 16 December – 1 February. The Easter Holiday period usually lasts ten days. The winter school holiday lasts for two weeks in July. There is also a spring school holiday from the last week of September to the second week of October.For detailed information on major festivals and events get a copy of *Great Events – Queensland* from the Queensland Events Corporation, PO Box 7990, Waterfront Place, Qld, 4001, tel: (073) 221 1552 fax: 221 1684.

• Coastal waters in summer are inhabited by sharks, box jellyfish and in the north, crocodiles.
• The state has deadly snakes. When in the bush wear boots, thick long socks and long trousers. Ticks and leeches are common so check your body thoroughly. Ticks can be dangerous; remove them with kerosene or methylated spirits (try not to break the body off leaving the head inside your body). Leeches can be removed with salt or heat.

The chance of being attacked, stung or bitten by venomous wildlife is remote but, if a poisonous snake or spider should bite, try to stay calm, wrap the the area in a tight bandage, as you would with a sprained ankle (*do not* use a tourniquet or suck out the poison), attach a splint to the limb, keep very still and send for help.

A similar procedure applies to poisonous marine life. Sea wasps are jellyfish which sting, causing welt marks. Douse the wound with vinegar and don't remove the stingers. Do not swim in unprotected waters.

Respect **fire bans** (broadcast on radio) and be careful with cigarette butts and broken glass which can ignite bushfires in hot, dry weather. If caught in a fire, head for a clearing (avoid dense tree growths). If in a car, get off the road, get under the dashboard and cover yourself, preferably with a blanket.

If bushwalking or camping, leave an itinerary with friends and go prepared for the possibility of getting lost. Remember that nights can be freezing despite high day temperature.

Health Services

Australia offers free service at public hospitals to its citizens and permanent residents, and has universal health care under **Medicare** system. This covers most of the cost of visiting a general practitioner, depending on whether the doctor uses bulk-billing practices. But these services only extend to citizens of the UK and New Zealand. Visitors must pay in full and up-front for dental treatment,

ambulance charges, and medicines. The cost of an unsubsidized, standard visit to a doctor is about A\$35, but serious illness can be more expensive. Traveller's insurance covering medical care and medicines is therefore highly recommended. A personal basic medical kit could also be a good idea.

Personal Safety

There are 6500 police in the state. In 1992–93 there were 254 homicides (93% solved) and 529 reported rapes and attempted rapes (81% led to prosecution).

Emergencies

The number for emergencies is **000** – for the police, ambulance and other emergency services. Crisis hotlines and interpreter services are listed at the front of the *White Pages* of the telephone directory. Directories also list emergency services.

Etiquette

Australians are mostly informal. The business community still wear suits, but in rural and suburban areas there is a high level of informality. Some hotels, restaurants and clubs have **dress codes**, but this is usually to ensure that people do not arrive in casual wear in the evening. Queenslanders will tell you what is appropriate.

Tipping: Tipping is not standard practice. You may wish to add 10% to the bill at a restaurant if you are impressed with the service. Restaurant prices carry no taxes and service charges. Food is of high quality and generally quite cheap.

Language

Australians speak English as their first language. While the country is committed to multiculturalism – which means that most major organisations will have translators and interpreters – in suburban and regional areas people who do not speak English will have some difficulty. Telstra offers an interpreter service: numbers are available in the *White Pages*.

Australian English inevitably has some local variations. To investigate Australian English further, read *Aussie Talk: The Macquarie Dictionary of Australian Colloquialisms* (1984) published by the Macquarie Library, Sydney.

GOOD READING

Famous works of fiction set in Queensland include:
• Patrick White (1976) *A Fringe of Leaves*, Jonathan Cape, UK.
• Xavier Herbert (1938) *Capricornia*, Angus & Robertson, Sydney.
• David Malouf (1991) *Remembering Babylon*, Random House, Sydney.
• Peter Carey (1981) *Bliss*, University of Queensland Press, St Lucia.
Non-fiction works include:
• David Colfelt (1995) *The Whitsunday Book*, Windward Publications, Berry NSW.
• Bruce Elder (1988) *Blood on the Wattle: The Massacres and Maltreatment of Aborigines since 1788*, New Holland, Sydney.
• Manning Clark (1963) *A Short History of Australia*, Penguin, Melbourne.
• Alan Moorehead (1963) *Cooper's Creek*, Penguin, Melbourne.

INDEX